FREEWAVE

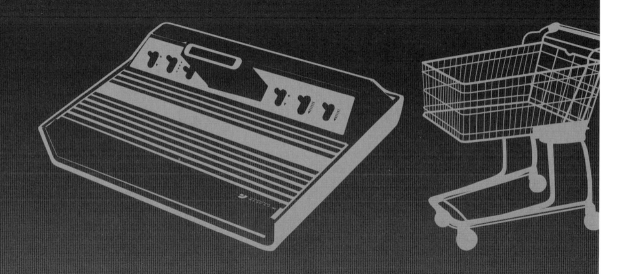

FREEWAVE

David Luscombe
Alison Roscoe
Edward Booth-Clibborn

"a scrapbook of
freeware for the
cut and paste
generation"

Max Kisman

copyright

First published in 2004 by Booth-Clibborn Editions
12 Percy Street / London W1T 1DW / www.booth-clibborn.com

Text copyright © David Luscombe, Alison Roscoe and Max Kisman
Design copyright © David Luscombe and all participants in the Freewave
project. David Luscombe has asserted his moral right under the Copyright,
Designs and Patents Act. 1988. to be identified as the author of this work.

Designed and created by David Luscombe
Project Managed by Alison Roscoe
Published by Edward Booth-Clibborn

The text, captions and artwork in this book have been supplied by their relative creators
and while every effort has been made to ensure accuracy, Booth-Clibborn Editions
cannot accept responsibility for errors or omissions under any circumstances.

We have made all reasonable efforts to reach designers and/or copyright owners of
images used in this book. We are prepared to pay fair and reasonable fees for any usage
made without compensation or agreement.

A Cataloguing-in-Publication record for this book is available from the Publisher.

ISBN 1 86154273-9

Printed and bound in China

contents

The square denotes the
section you are in. The
number pronounces the
page you are looking at.
The words show the gallery
section you shall proceed
through. One gallery after
another until you are faced
with the people within.

FONTWARE

007 QUIQUE OLLERVIDES EMAIL: QUIQUE@HULLAHULLA.COM.MX

RESPONSE

ONCE DOWN THERE, ALL SOUNDS
ARE CUT OFF. OVERHEAD TRAVEL
PATHS VANISH IN THE THIN AIR.
MOTORISED RIVER NOISES CRUMBLE
AWAY. MOVING AT A STEADY PACE,
THE SILENCE OVERWHELMS. ONLY
THE SOUND OF BREATHING AND THE
SCRAPING STEPS ON THE TRAIL.
EVERYTHING IS GONE. NO BIRDS,
NO HUMANS, NO CARS, NO CITIES.
A BREEZE CAUSES A SHIVER. THE
SILENCE RUNS DOWN THE SPINE.
THEN, BACK ON THE HILLTOP,
THE SILENCE IS GONE.

ACERINA ABC123 NOW NOW on

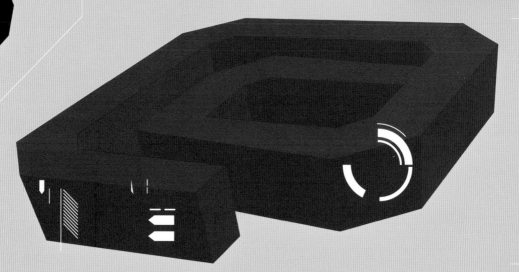

ABCDEFGHIJKLMNOPQRSTUVWXYZ
0123456789!£$%&*()@?/#~[]{}

 QUIQUE OLLERVIDES. **EMAIL:** QUIQUE@HULAHULA.COM.MX

Takasan

Quique Ollervides

ABCDEFGHIJ
0123456789.

Takasan: A to J / 0 to 9 / Uppercase = 48pt

abcdefghijklmnopqrstuvwxyz
0123456789

Takasan: Alphabet / Lowercase = 14pt

(){}[]
!#&%&3° òÑ/¿?.-ə()~

Takasan: Ampersand = 400pt

&04

abc123

Takasan: abc123 = 150pt

PLay

Takasan: Play = 150pt

Tabique

Quique Ollervides

abcdefghijkl
mnopqrstu
uwxyzo1234
56789!£$%&
*()@?/\#[]{}

Tabique: Alphabet / Numbers / Symbols / Lowercase = 24pt

fierros

Quique Ollervides

Fierros: No / Lowercase = 72pt

Fierros: Alphabet / Numbers / Lowercase = 20pt

Quique Ollervides

Mutis: abc12 = 70pt

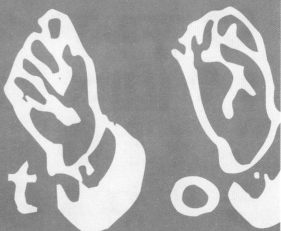

Mutis: Inside = 110pt

Mutis: To = 240pt

Mutis: Alphabet / Numbers / Lowercase = 18pt

1. Ahorre pilas

KO!

vol

pitoenpozo®

2. Cuide sus pertenencias

SMILE

doma

WANTED

METAL MICKEY

METAL MICKEY FONT
PROJECT MADE POSSIBLE BY:

Metal Mickey Dingbat is designed by Rebel One®
Visit www.Rebelone.Net for more information
Copyright © 2004. Rebel One®

REBEL ONE

019 PATRICK TAN · EMAIL: INFO@REBELONE.NET

In this book only

SHAMPLE

A FREE BITE OF THIS TASTY NEW FONT

SHAMROCKING.COM

King-o-Type

SPINOUT **Good Rockin'**
SPINOFF **KINGU SAN**
FIRSTY
THE **EZ** WAY **COMEBACK**
Admiradores
KING CREOLE
Girls! **HARUM SCARUM**
Kissin' COUSINS
K·C·Alternate **G·I·BLUES**

01

BY SHAMROCK MM

Shamrock

SHIT

QUAMODQUE

FREE ON MY SITE:
Putain

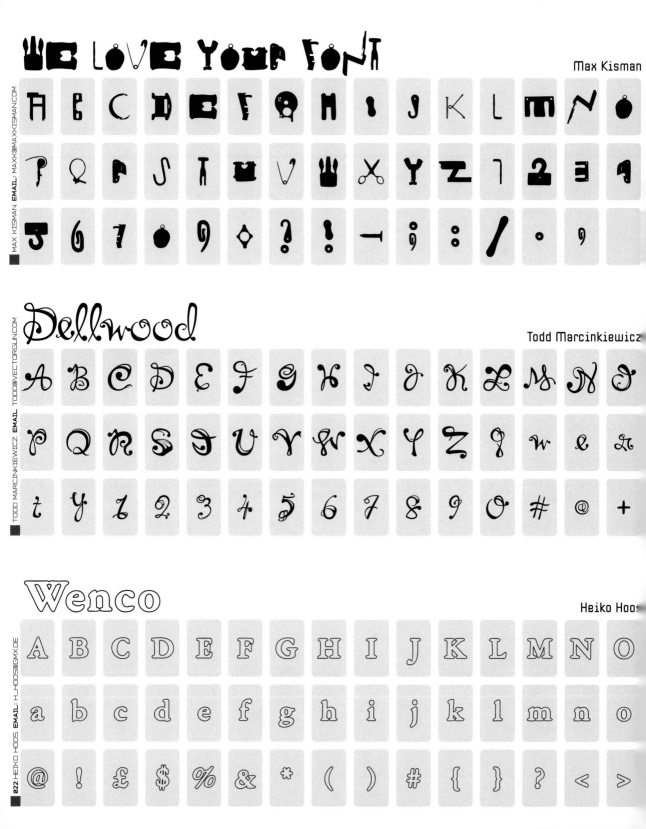

WE LOVE YOUR FONT

Max Kisman

Dellwood

Todd Marcinkiewicz

Wenco

Heiko Hoos

Dan Smith

Dan Smith

Angel Dust

Boris Dworschak

A B C D E F G H I J K L M N O

a b c d e f g h i j k l m n o

1 2 3 4 5 6 7 8 9 0 &))) # ? $

DANIEL SMITH EMAIL: OSHIMASH@HOTMAIL.COM

DANIEL SMITH EMAIL: INFO@REVSKIN.DE

023 BORIS DWORSCHAK EMAIL: BORIS@ECHOBASE.INFO

A	Mike Abbink	(mike@abbink.biz)
B	Mr. Keedy	(ciphertype@aol.com)
C	John Bielenberg and Doug Raphael	(info@c2llc.com)
D	Michael Bartalos	(mb@bartalos.com)
E	Adam Brodsley and Eric Heiman	(info@volumesf.com)
F	Edward Fella	(CalArts School of Art)
G	Joshua Distler	(mail@shiftype.com)
H	Jim Parkinson	(parkinson@typedesign.com)
I	Rudy Vanderlans	(editor@emigre.com)
J	John Harsey	(john@hersey.com)
K	Bob Aufuldish	(bob@fontBoy.com)
L	Peter Lofting	(lofting@apple.com)
M	Joe Kral	(info@testpilotcollective.com)
N	Joachim Müller-Lancé	(joachim@kamedesign.com)
O	Jean-Benoit Lévy and Claudia Dallendörfer	(usa@and.ch)
P	Rodrigo Cavazos and Stefan Hattenbach	(info@psyops.com)
Q	Mike Kohnke	(mike@typebox.com)
R	Delve Withrington	(delve@mediarts.com)
S	G. Dan Covert	(urbansoul@mac.com)
T	Alastair Johnston	(www.poltroonpress.com)
U	Erik Adigard	(adigard@madxs.com)
V	Joe VanDerBos	(joe@joevanderbos.com)
W	Mark Winn	(mark@vehiclesf.com)
X	Mark Fox	(mfox@blackdog.com)
Y	Max Kisman	(info@hollandfonts.com)
Z	Zuzana Licko	(editor@emigre.com)
0-5,7,8	Erik Spiekerman	(erik@uniteddesigners.com)
6,9	Sumner Stone	(sstone@stonetypefoundry.com)
&	David Lance Goines	(dlg@goines.net)
<>,.={}[]	Dennis Pasco	(dpasco@pixeltan.net)
_-:;|\!?/˜	Richard Chang	(richard@grand-opening.net)

001

001

006

006

011

011

016

016

021

021

026

026

027

028

029

029

030

030

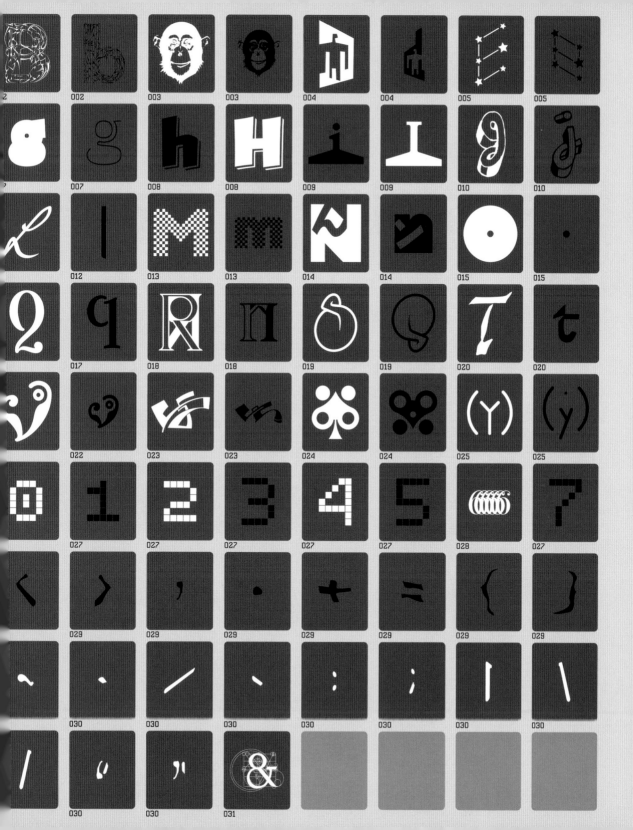

Revolution

A definition of typography is obsolete. The institution of type is abolished. Its power is defeated. Since its official manifestation, type has been outlawed. Type is nothing more than a tone, a sound, a noise. Parts and details are ticks, spurts and vibrations. Letters, glyphs or characters

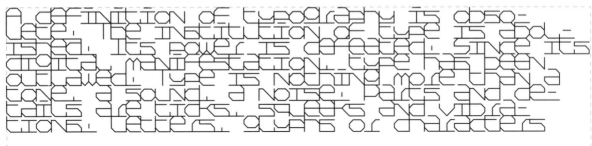

have lost their intentional meaning and became transient notations. New forms will be defined by the remix.

026/027 MAX KISMAN EMAIL: MAXK@MAXKISMAN.COM

Depending on the time, place and tools, any idea will find a specific form. An image can only look the way it is at the moment of its appearance. There is always a particular and suitable way for individual expression to communicate.

Expression of Language depends on the need to use it.

Articulate. Visual articulation is a downright representation of meaning.

articulate

monotalk

monotalk

It is the precipitation of a process on a specific moment, an enumeration of vision and opinion, relevance of purpose, cultural reference, experience and insights, and the exploration of freedom, within limitations of time, production and techniques.

MONOTALK BY MAX KISMAN

NARROW8

Stefanie Koerner

a b c d e f g h i j
k l m n o p q r s t
u v w x y z A B C D
E F G H I J K L M N
O P Q R S T U V W X
Y Z 1 2 3 4 5 6 7 8
9 0 ! " £ $ % ^ & *
( ) - + • = [ ] { }
¡ : ; @ ' / < > ?
| \ # ~

Plakken★   Stefanie Koerner

a b c d e f g h i j
k l m n o p q r s t
u v w x y z A B C D
E F G H I J K L M N
O P Q R S T U V W X
Y Z 1 2 3 4 5 6 7 8
9 0 ! " % & ★ ( ) +
= - [ ] ( ) ' • - /
\ ? @ • # : ¡

★RVP

Base-PP

ABCDEFGHIJKLMNOPQRSTU abcdefghijklmnopqrstuvwxyz1234567890!"#$%&'()*+,-./:;<=>?@[\]^_`{|}~

RICARDO RUIZ
HTTP://BASEV.HAS.IT

GATO ESCALDADA

GATO ESCALDADA

1234567890

ABCDEFGHIJKLMNOPQRSTUVWXYZ

!"£$%&*<>_+=—'@#;:/?,.

aA aA abc **abc**

bB bB def **def**

cC cC

ill photography: Jake Tilson. Overlay Pattern used on montages: Kjetil Vatne

dD dD ijk

eE eE no**mno**

fF fF pqr**pqr**

nts used on this page: Neco and Maquinamario by BaseV

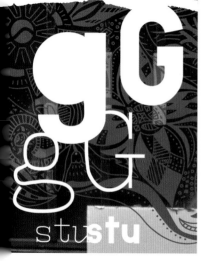

gG gG stu**stu**

hH hH vwx**vwx**

iI iI yz**yz**

HUMAN
SUSANA SIMPLICIO
BACKGROUND IMAGE: BORIS SAVIC

Taro Yamakawa
EDDIE

033 TARO YAMAKAWA **EMAIL:** TAROUT@TAROUT.NET

MASTER

ABCDEFGHIJKLMNOPQRSTUVWXYZ

ABCDEFGHIJKLMNOPQRSTUVWXYZ

0123456789àáäüæ?!/$€×''''.:;¡+†=-—"

MASTER REGULAR/21 POINTS:

BLACK METAL, DEATH METAL, GOTHIC METAL, DOOM METAL, THRASH, SPEED METAL, POWER METAL, PROGRESSIVE METAL, HEAVY METAL AND GRINDCORE.

MASTER REGULAR ITALIC/21 POINTS:

SMOKE, EXPLOSIONS, STACKS OF AMPLIFIERS, SPANDEX, BEER, LEATHER, LONG HAIR, LOTS AND LOTS OF BEAUTIFUL WOMEN AND, OF COURSE, BLISTERING GUITAR ATTACKS. METAL MUSIC IS A UNIQUE ARTFORM ALL ON ITS OWN.

MASTER REGULAR/12 POINTS:

BLACK METAL, DEATH METAL, GOTHIC METAL, DOOM METAL, THRASH, SPEED METAL, POWER METAL, PROGRESSIVE METAL, HEAVY METAL AND GRINDCORE.

MASTER REGULAR ITALIC/12 POINTS:

SMOKE, EXPLOSIONS, STACKS OF AMPLIFIERS, SPANDEX, BEER, LEATHER, LONG HAIR, LOTS AND LOTS OF BEAUTIFUL WOMEN AND, OF COURSE, BLISTERING GUITAR ATTACKS. METAL MUSIC IS A UNIQUE ARTFORM ALL ON ITS OWN.

+a free airguitar!!!

BANG YOUR HEAD!!

homage to a levitating marquee

hyperalpha tubular data format
getting the message through without any
pain or suffering to large colourful birds

036/037 DAVID LUSCOMBE EMAIL: DAVE@FONTMONSTER.ORG

I LOVE

HOME

ONCE DOWN
THERE ALL
SOUNDS ARE
CUT OFF

ABC

ABCDEFGHIJKLMNOPQRSTUVWXYZ

ABCDEFGHIJKLMNOPQRSTUVWXYZ

From an internal **view** point observing its motion. **It** all starts **with** the initial Its **initial** balance. position. **Placing** the point of gravity right **there**, where its **power** Stretches **in** an upward **motion.**

mutagen

ABCDEFGHIJKLMNOPQRSTUVWXYZ
1234567890!£$%&(){}[]@?<>/\

PHOTOS: J STRATEN **EMAIL:** INFO@JOERNSTRATEN.COM

EMAIL: CONTACT@NLFMAGAZINE.COM

SCRATCHWARE: NLF MAGAZINE

EMAIL: DAVE@FONTMONSTER.ORG

038/039 DAVID LUSCOMBE

WIDE8

STEFANIE KOERNER
BACKGROUND IMAGE:
BJORN HANSEN / DAVID LUSCOMBE

Execution

When the space is empty,
the mind is blank.
Anything can happen. Good things,
bad things. Whatever it will be,
it doesn't really matter.
What does matter is that it happens.
The first draw is the hardest. Everything
else must be as decisive and as accurate.
The image will build up to its completion.
Perfection is in the execution of stopping■

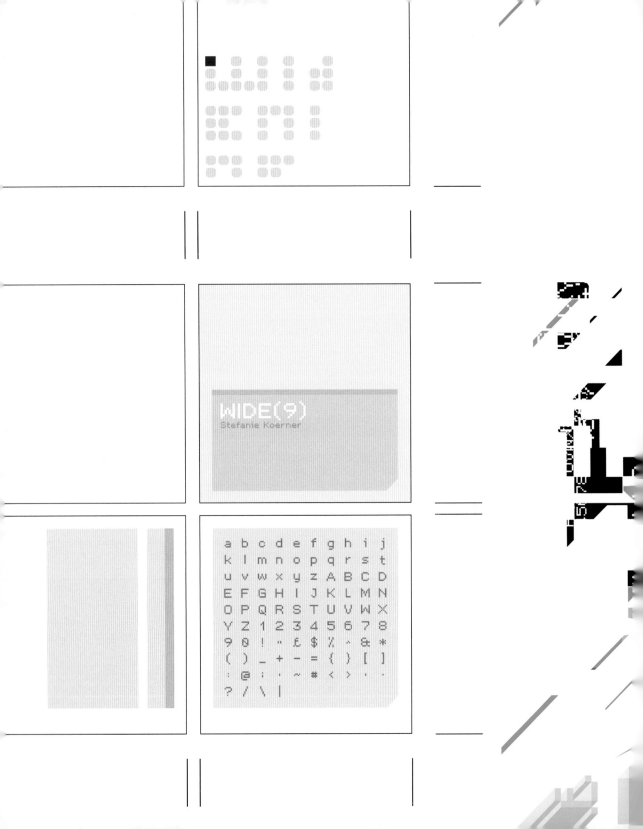

WIDE(9)

Stefanie Koerner

a b c d e f g h i j
k l m n o p q r s t
u v w x y z A B C D
E F G H I J K L M N
O P Q R S T U V W X
Y Z 1 2 3 4 5 6 7 8
9 0 ! " £ $ % ^ & *
( ) _ + - = { } [ ]
: @ ; ' ~ # < > . ,
? / \ |

 STEFANIE KOERNER **EMAIL:** MONOCHROM@GMX.DE

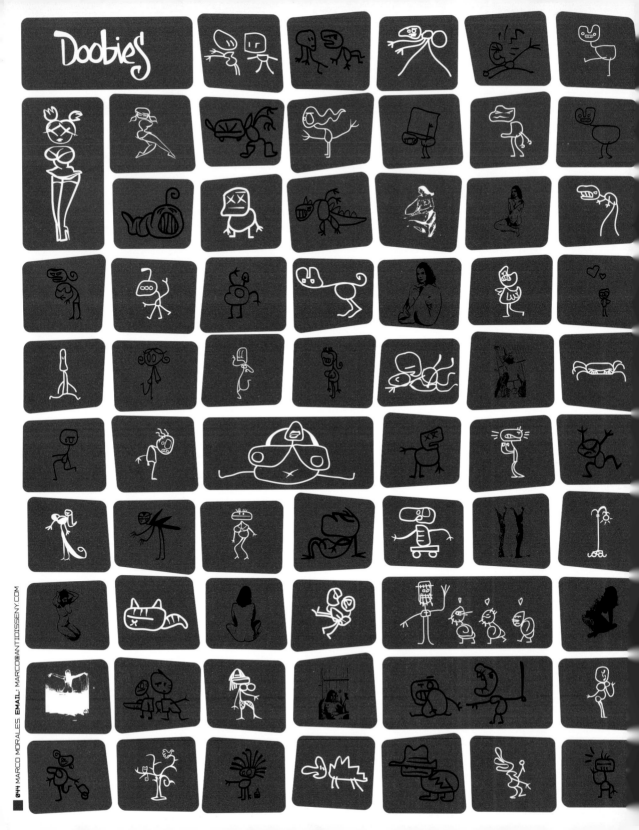

LOADED
BY ANDREW WILSON

TODAY'S LOWERCASE, TOMORROW'S UPPERCASE.

ABCDEFGHIJKLMNOPQRSTUVWXYZ
1234567890!"$%^&*()_+-=() @:#?/\

045 ANDREW WILSON EMAIL: F9@FILTER9.COM

GAUGHENAR
BLOB
PONEY
CLUB
HAMBURG
QWERTY

vectorkit

gratis

THE PHONO ART ENSEMBLE

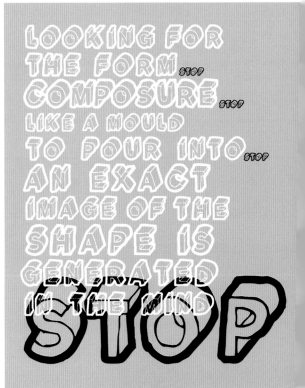

LOOKING FOR
THE FORM stop
COMPOSURE stop
LIKE A MOULD
TO POUR INTO stop
AN EXACT
IMAGE OF THE
SHAPE IS
GENERATED
IN THE MIND
STOP

Instructions : compose words with letters.

BUBBLE

ABCDEFGHIJKLMNO
PQRSTUVWXYZ

INDUS

A3CDEFGHIJKLMNOP RS
TUVWXYZ

BOXES

ABCDEFGHIJ
KLMNOPQRST
UVWXYZ

**TROISDE
PLEIN**

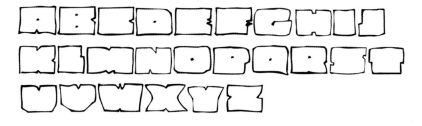

ABCDEFGHIJKLMNO
PQRSTUVWXYZ

TROISDE

ABCDEFGHIJKLMNO
PQRSTUVWXYZ

angryblue
controlled

Abc defghij klmnopqrstuvwxyz

When the space is empty the mind is blank
Anything can happen. Good things bad things
Whatever it will be it doesn't really matter.
What does matter is that it happens.
The first draw is the hardest. Everything else
must be as decisive and as accurate.
The image will build up to its completion.
Perfection is in the execution of stopping.

Once down there, all sounds are cut off.
Overhead travel paths vanish in the thin air.
Motorised river noises crumple away. Moving
at a steady pace the silence overwhelms.
Only the sound of breathing and the scraping
steps on the trail. Everything is gone.
No birds no humans no cars no cities.
A breeze causes a shiver. The silence runs
down the spine. Then, back on the hilltop
the silence is gone.

Flattening out with a circular stroke
For a millisecond the eye meets the
contact point of energiser and energised
The diagonal shift will securely strike the
premeditated target.

ABCDEFGHIJKLMNOPQRSTUVWXYZ

WHEN THE SPACE IS EMPTY. THE MIND IS BLANK. ANYTHING CAN HAPPEN. GOOD THINGS BAD THINGS
WHATEVER IT WILL BE, IT DOESN'T REALLY MATTER. WHAT DOES MATTER IS THAT IT HAPPENS.
THE FIRST DRAW IS THE HARDEST. EVERYTHING ELSE MUST BE AS DECISIVE AND AS ACCURATE.
THE IMAGE WILL BUILD UP TO ITS COMPLETION. PERFECTION IS IN THE EXECUTION OF STOPPING.

ONCE DOWN THERE, ALL SOUNDS ARE CUT OFF. OVERHEAD TRAVEL PATHS VANISH IN THE THIN AIR.
MOTORISED RIVER NOISES CRUMPLE AWAY. MOVING AT A STEADY PACE THE SILENCE OVERWHELMS.
ONLY THE SOUND OF BREATHING AND THE SCRAPING STEPS ON THE TRAIL. EVERYTHING IS GONE.
NO BIRDS NO HUMANS NO CARS NO CITIES. A BREEZE CAUSES A SHIVER. THE SILENCE RUNS
DOWN THE SPINE THEN BACK ON THE HILLTOP. THE SILENCE IS GONE.

FLATTENING OUT WITH A CIRCULAR STROKE. FOR A MILLISECOND THE EYE MEETS THE
CONTACT POINT OF ENERGISER AND ENERGISED. THE DIAGONAL SHIFT WILL SECURELY STRIKE THE
PREMEDITATED TARGET.

ANGRYBLUE

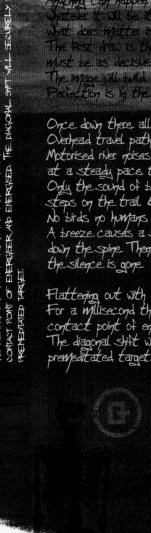

vectorware

DIFFERENT
OUTWARDLY BUT SIMILAR ON THE INSIDE

051 DAVID LUSCOMBE **EMAIL:** DAVE@FONTMONSTER.ORG

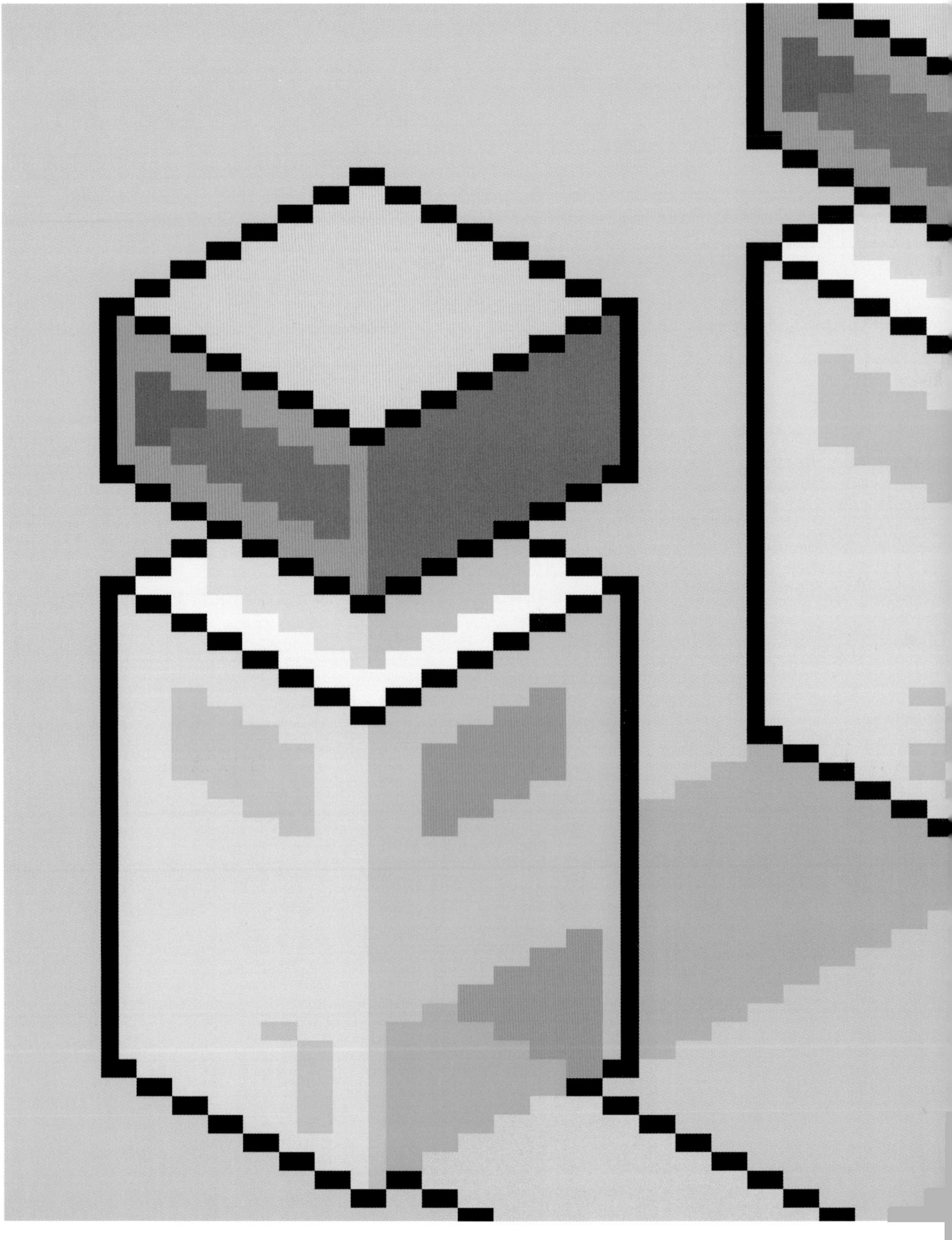

SIMILAR
OUTWARDLY BUT DIFFERENT ON THE INSIDE

Errors break down the predictable, the expected and the obvious.

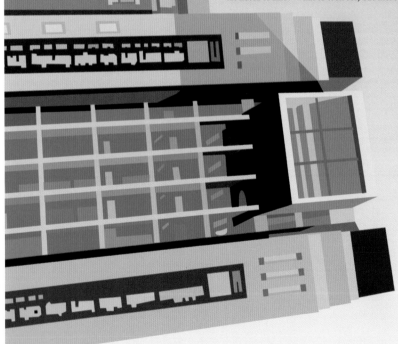

Quality

The quality of talent lies within its limitations, not within its possibilities. Dealing with physical limitations and reality, the professional designer often has to be inventive and improvise to solve a problem within a limited timeframe. He needs to be practical and efficient. **He needs to know what to look for, but more importantly, when to stop.**

Max Kisman 2004

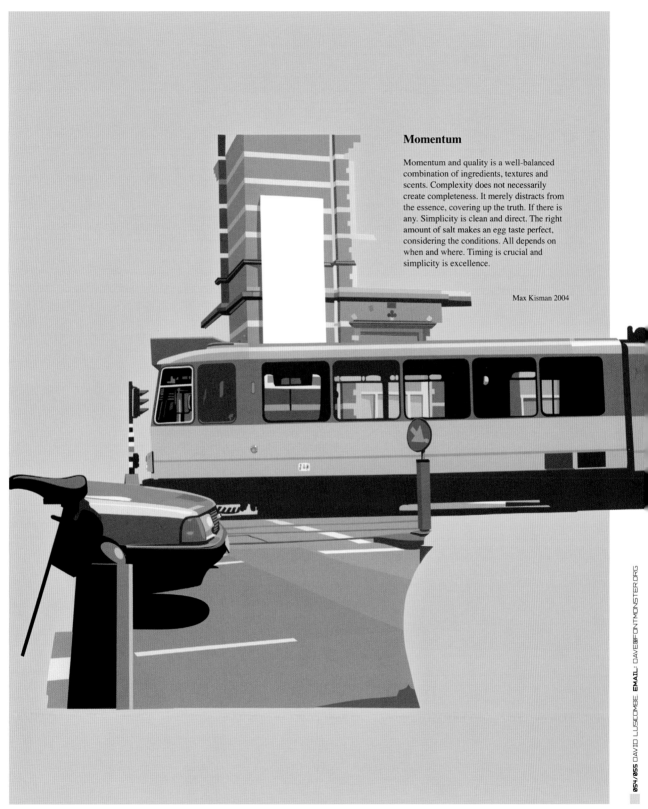

Momentum

Momentum and quality is a well-balanced combination of ingredients, textures and scents. Complexity does not necessarily create completeness. It merely distracts from the essence, covering up the truth. If there is any. Simplicity is clean and direct. The right amount of salt makes an egg taste perfect, considering the conditions. All depends on when and where. Timing is crucial and simplicity is excellence.

Max Kisman 2004

An error is not necessarily a failure. With errors the unforeseen results will be surprising and might have an even stronger impact. Errors confront us with the physical and mental limitations of possibilities. There is a beauty in errors, as they shift reality from its predefined conditions and conventions. Errors are the beauty of imperfectness.

Max Kisman 2004

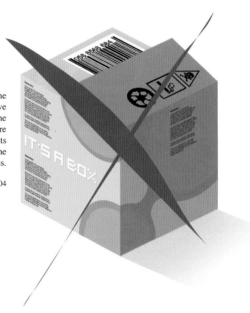

 DAVID LUSCOMBE **EMAIL:** DAVE@FONTMONSTER.ORG

Pixelfucker

UEKTORISM

REUSEABLE OBJECTS

VEKTORISM: Reusable Objects

The very idea of this set of graphics is to create reusable vector objects which can be used freely for other artworks or graphical layouts. All of the graphics in this section are created in such a way that other colours and/or modifications can be applied to the original vector works. The coloured dots at the corner of each object box represent colour varients available for that particular graphic.

ยักษ์

ยงเกียรติ กาญจนพายัพ

᪖

Pixel fucker

Yongkiat Karnchanapayap

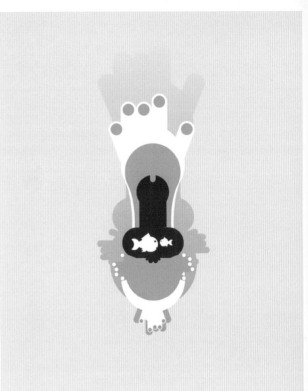

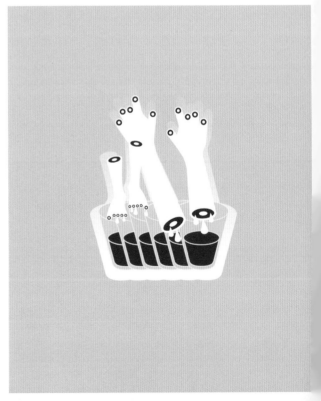

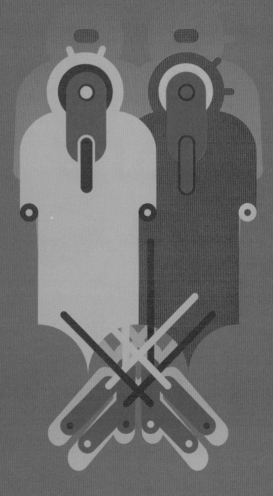

 SANTIAGO MORILLA **EMAIL:** SANTI@RETROVISOR.COM

FRAGILE
HANDLE WITH CARE

judo

and harmony for mankind
and harmony for mankind

pLANET
OF THE pHUNK

steepwaker

pHUNK

06V/065 PHUNK STUDIO EMAIL: ALVIN@PHUNKSTUDIO.COM

STEAL THIS POSTER
STEALING FROM THIEVES
DESIGN TO BREAK RULES

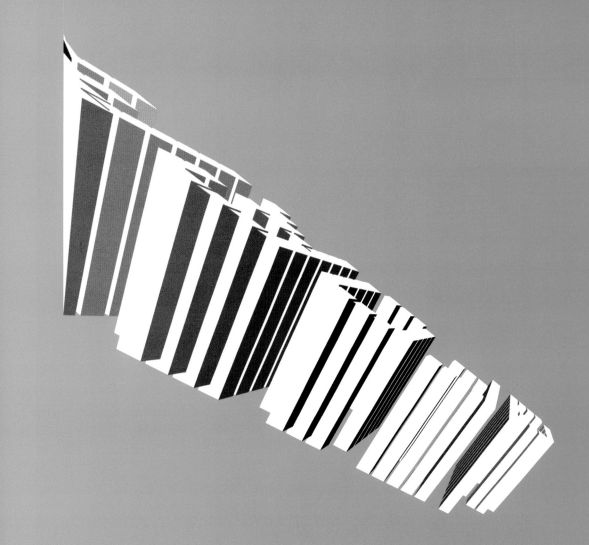

GUILLAUME DURAND **EMAIL:** DGEZED@ALV-H-EOL.NET

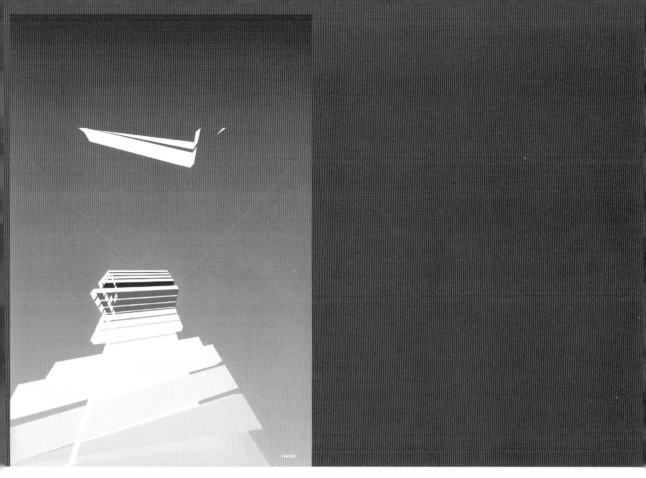

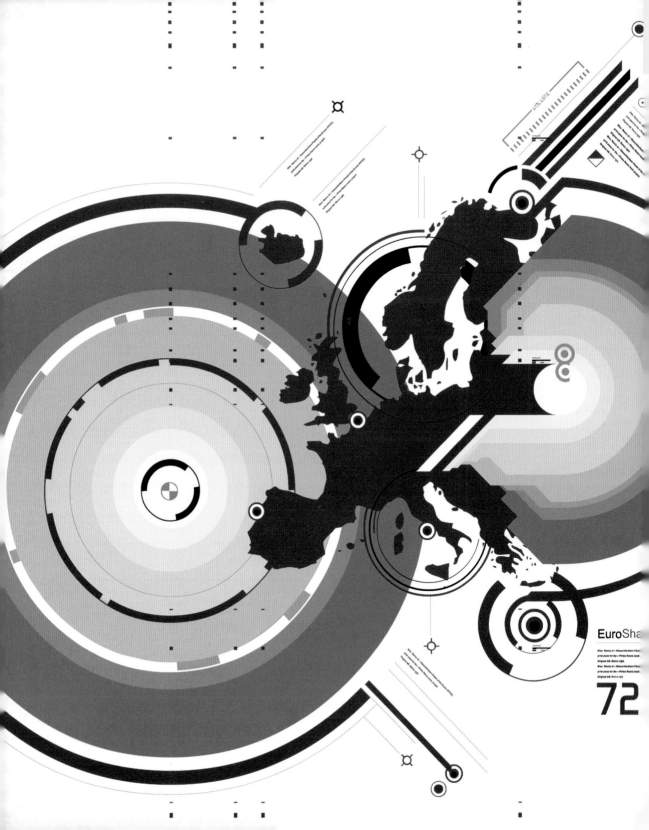

EuroSha

72

726

EuroShape

at. n° 02-a225

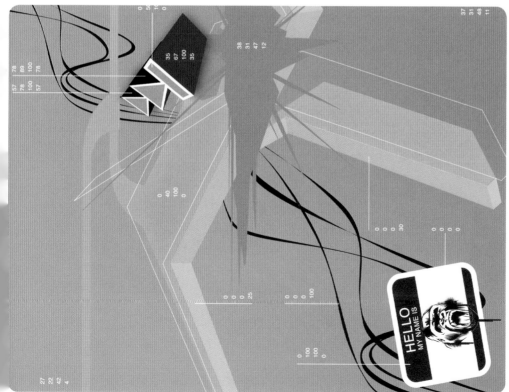

 MASA. EMAIL: INFO@MASA.COM.VE

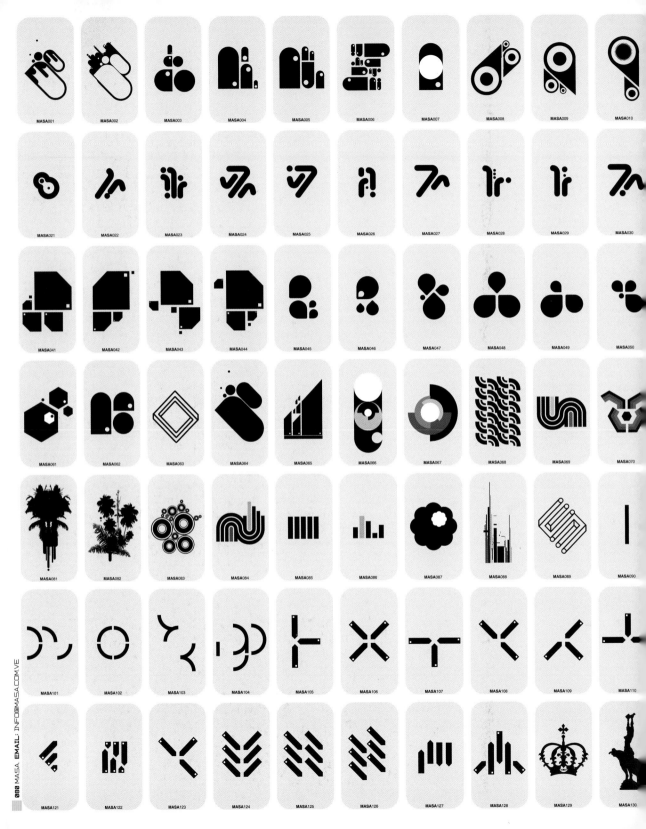

MASA001 MASA002 MASA003 MASA004 MASA005 MASA006 MASA007 MASA008 MASA009 MASA010

MASA021 MASA022 MASA023 MASA024 MASA025 MASA026 MASA027 MASA028 MASA029 MASA030

MASA041 MASA042 MASA043 MASA044 MASA045 MASA046 MASA047 MASA048 MASA049 MASA050

MASA061 MASA062 MASA063 MASA064 MASA065 MASA066 MASA067 MASA068 MASA069 MASA070

MASA081 MASA082 MASA083 MASA084 MASA085 MASA086 MASA087 MASA088 MASA089 MASA090

MASA101 MASA102 MASA103 MASA104 MASA105 MASA106 MASA107 MASA108 MASA109 MASA110

MASA121 MASA122 MASA123 MASA124 MASA125 MASA126 MASA127 MASA128 MASA129 MASA130

MASA011 MASA012 MASA013 MASA014 MASA015 MASA016 MASA017 MASA018 MASA019 MASA020

MASA031 MASA032 MASA033 MASA034 MASA035 MASA036 MASA037 MASA038 MASA039 MASA040

MASA051 MASA052 MASA053 MASA054 MASA055 MASA056 MASA057 MASA058 MASA059 MASA060

MASA071 MASA072 MASA073 MASA074 MASA075 MASA076 MASA077 MASA078 MASA079 MASA080

MASA091 MASA092 MASA093 MASA094 MASA095 MASA096 MASA097 MASA098 MASA099 MASA100

MASA111 MASA112 MASA113 MASA114 MASA115 MASA116 MASA117 MASA118 MASA119 MASA120

MASA131 MASA132 MASA133 MASA134 MASA135 MASA136 MASA137

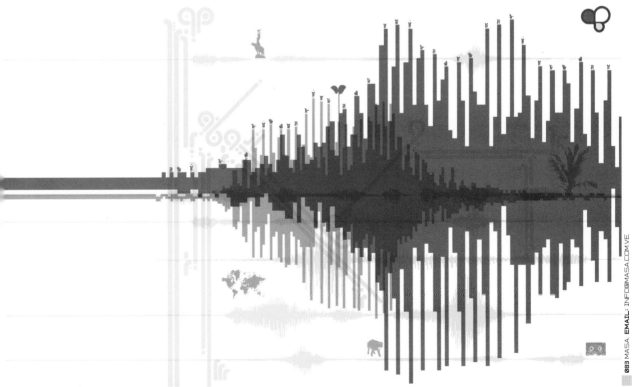

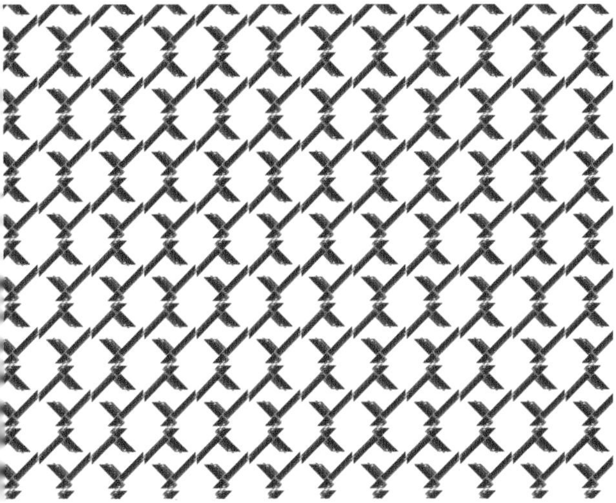

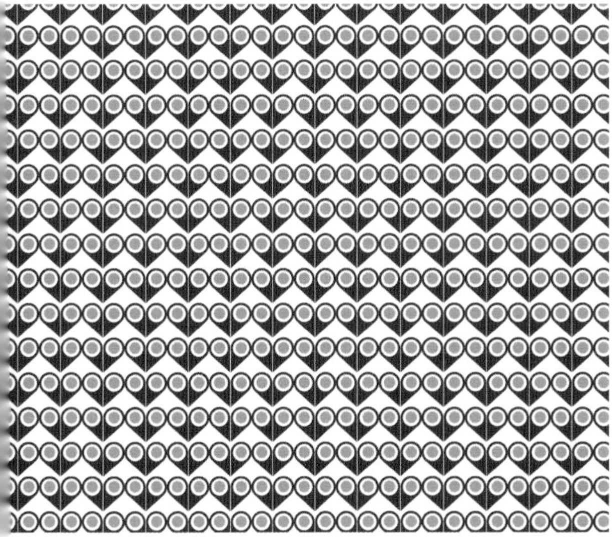

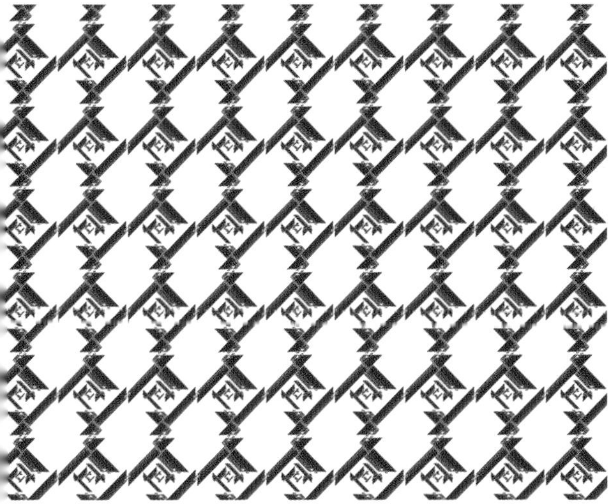

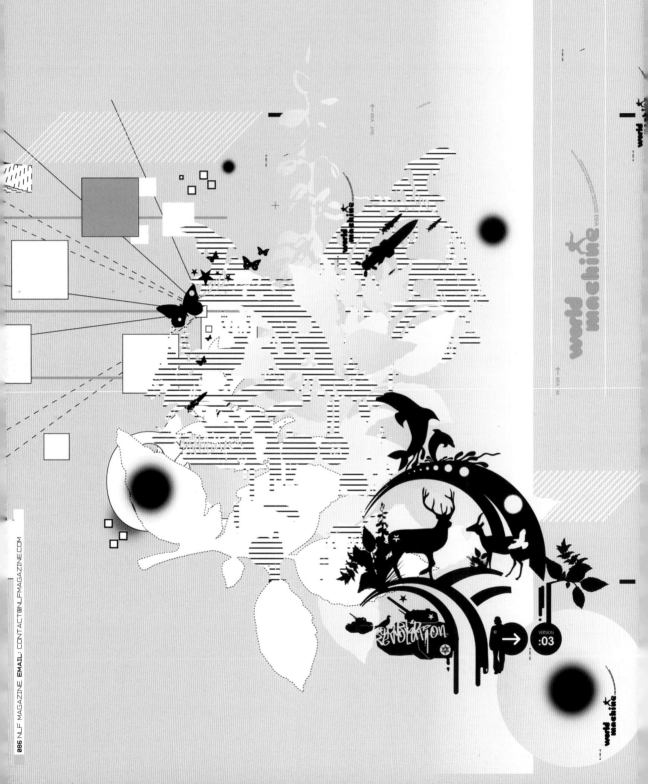

VERSION :03

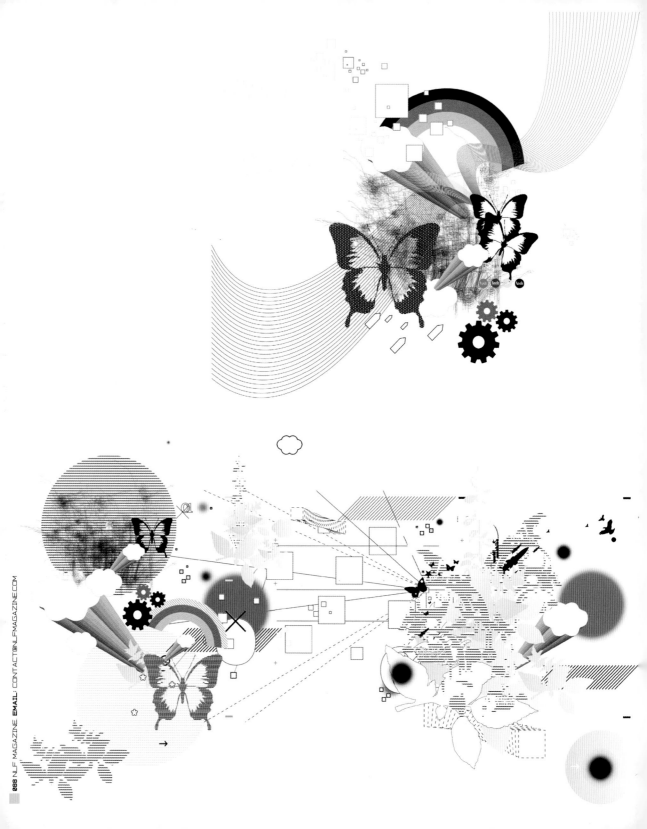

THIS WAY

IN _ V:03 →

OUT _ V:03 →

world machine™ V:03

EMAIL: CONTACT@NLFMAGAZINE.COM

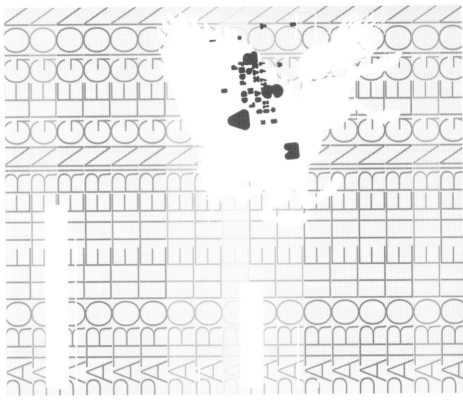

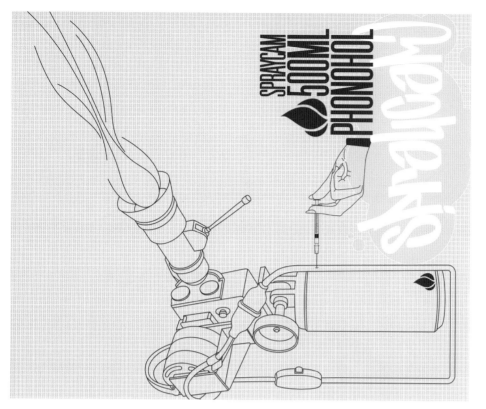

MISS KITTIN DROVE OUR NIGHT WILD
(DJ POGOSHELTER REMIX)

+69%

+46%

+23%

(HUMAN:GRID)

thinkfree

ANDREA VOLPICELLI _ EMAIL: ANDREA@ANDREAVOLPICELLI.COM

DEVOJČICA?

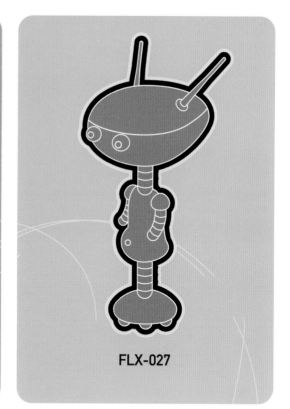

FLX-027

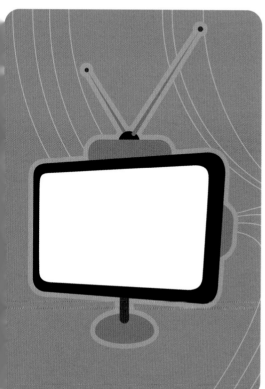

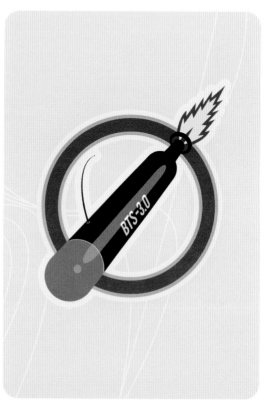

BTS-3.0

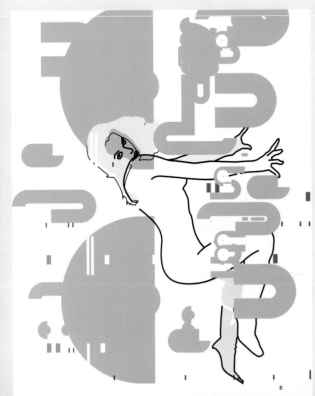

rinse
deluxe item

and then put a little bit of text in here
this line should be slightly longer than the first
make this short

keep clean

clean

keep clean

keep clean

and then put a little bit of text in here
this line should be slightly longer than
the first make this short

keep full

clean

again

put a little bit
of white text in here

put a little bit
of white text in here

Here's a one short line

again you got something here

AND YOU MIGHT
READ THIS

put a little bit
of white text in here

out
in

put a little bit
of white text in here

and then put a little bit of text in here
this line should be slightly longer than the first
make this short

put a little bit
of white text in here

build&copy
an all round
snatch total
rip

and then put a little bit of text in here
this line should be slightly longer than the first
make this short

and then put a little bit of text in here
this line should be slightly longer than the first
make this short

make this short   make

   Here's a one short line with icons

096/097 MARCO ALESSI EMAIL: INFO@FLOORLESS.COM

FUTURE VISION

Base 1 2 3 4 5

RUSSELL TATE
ILLUSTRATION

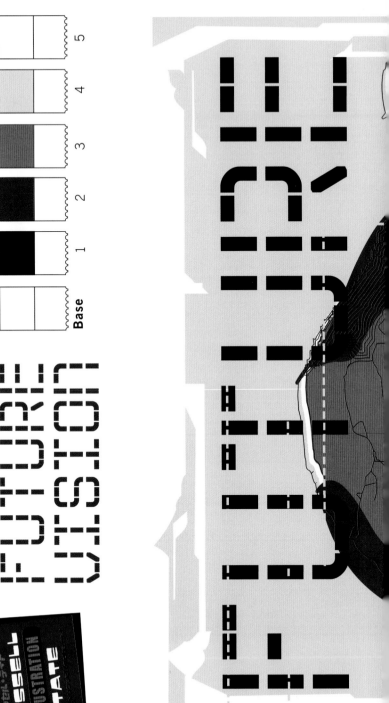

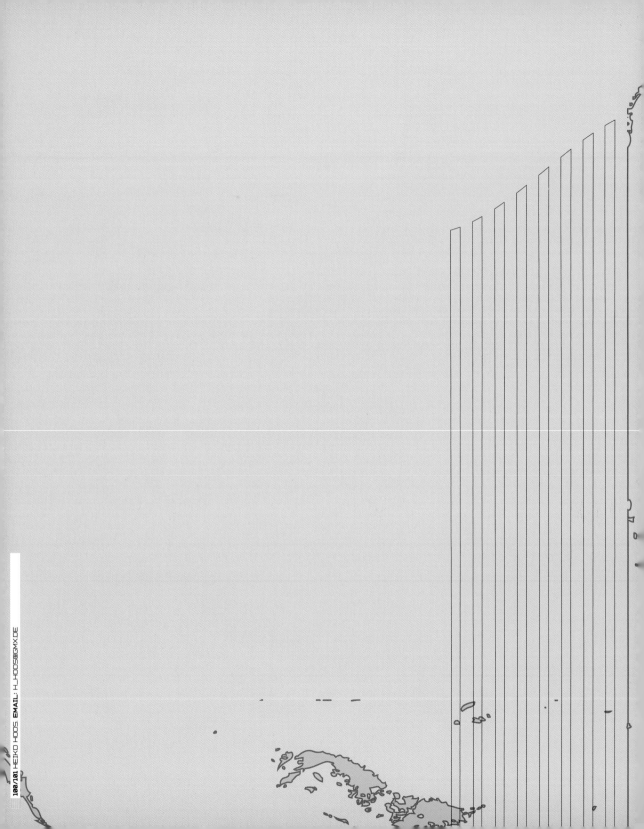

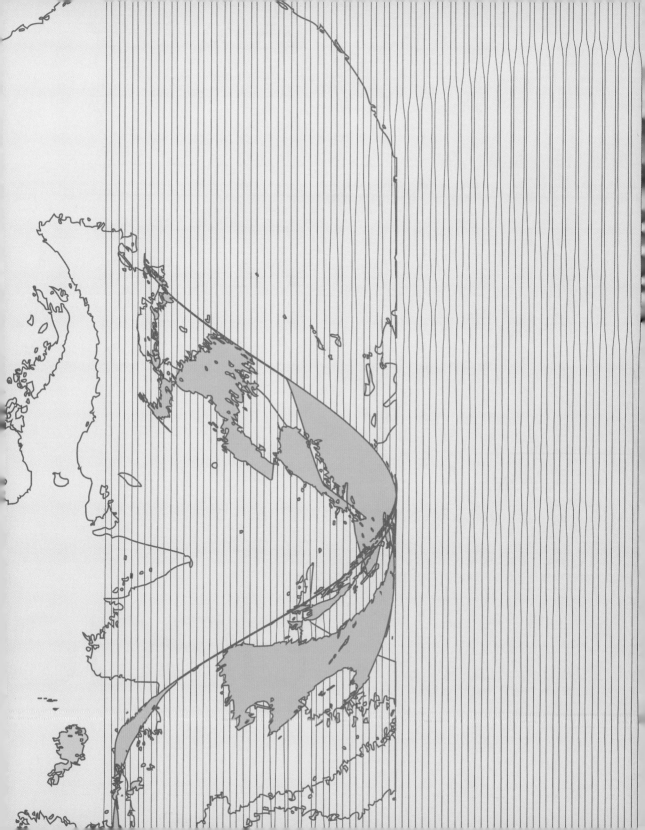

dead

HUMANWARE

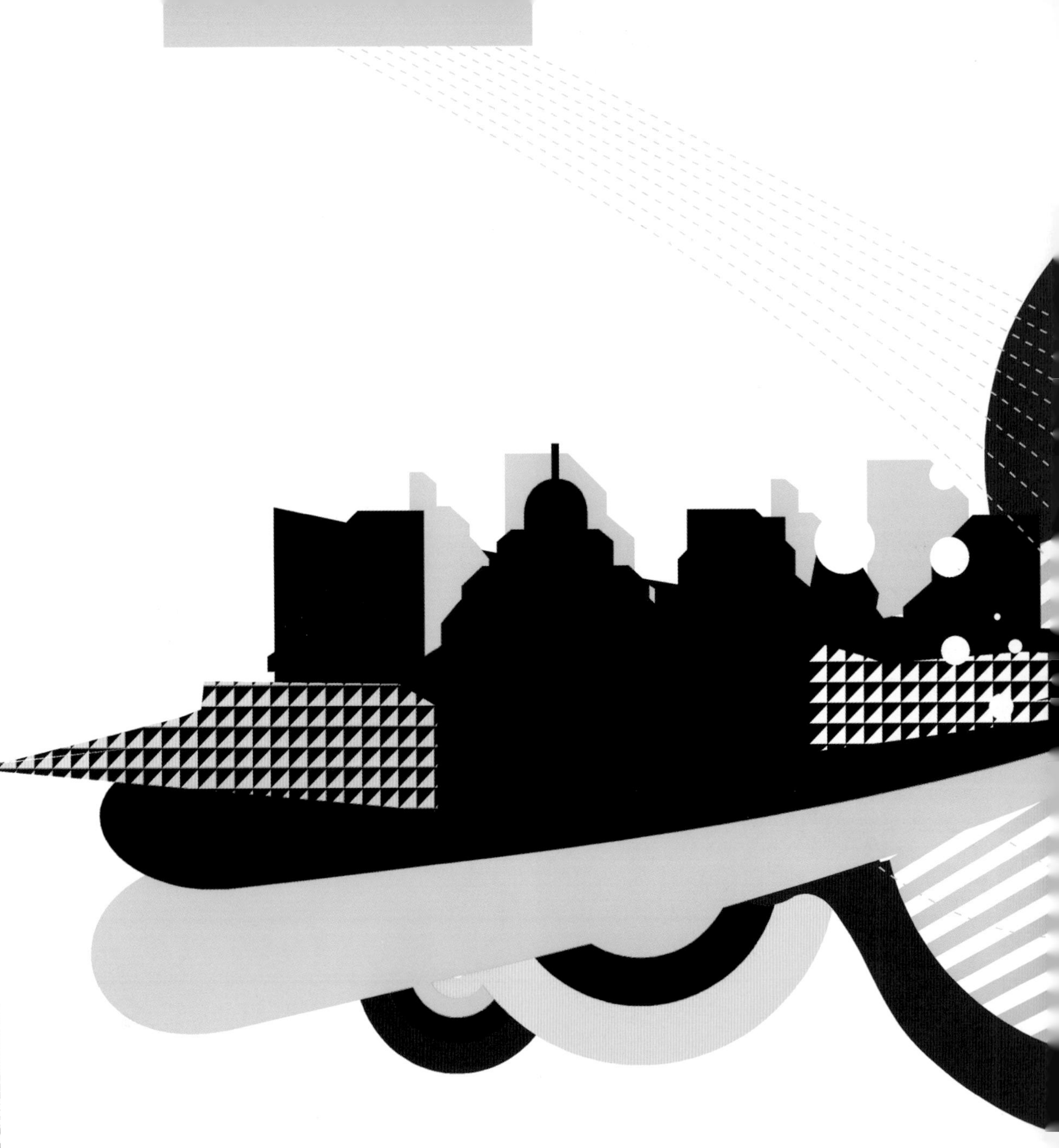

 YONGKIAT KARICHANAPAYAP **EMAIL:** YONGKIATK@PIXELFUCKER.NET

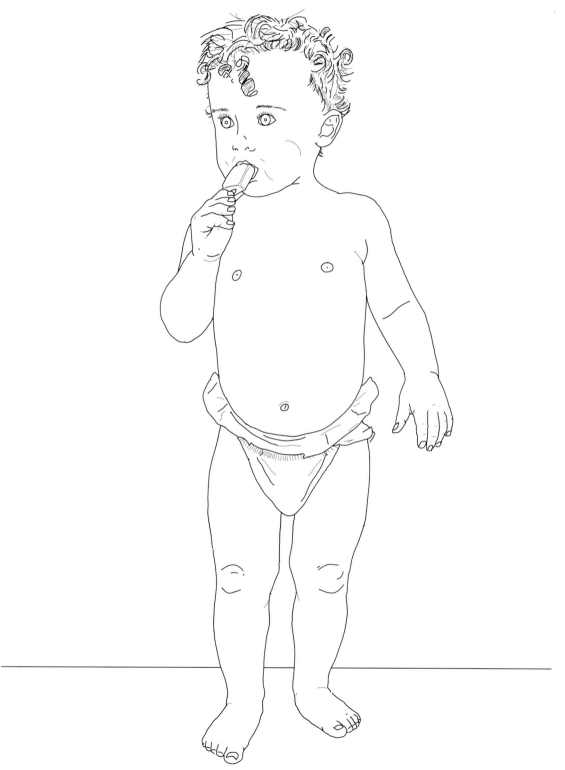

PUT YOUR
GRAPHIC HERE

GABRIEL SUCHOWOLSKI **EMAIL**: INFO@MICROBIANS.COM

ADAM HAYES **EMAIL**: ADAM@IDENTIKAL.COM

CAUTION:
THIS IS NOT
A REAL GRAFFITI!
IT IS A FAKE
VECTOR BASED
GRAFFITI PIECE.
ENJOY THE
CATHERINE
INFLATE TYPE.
YOUR CEER

sub-humanware

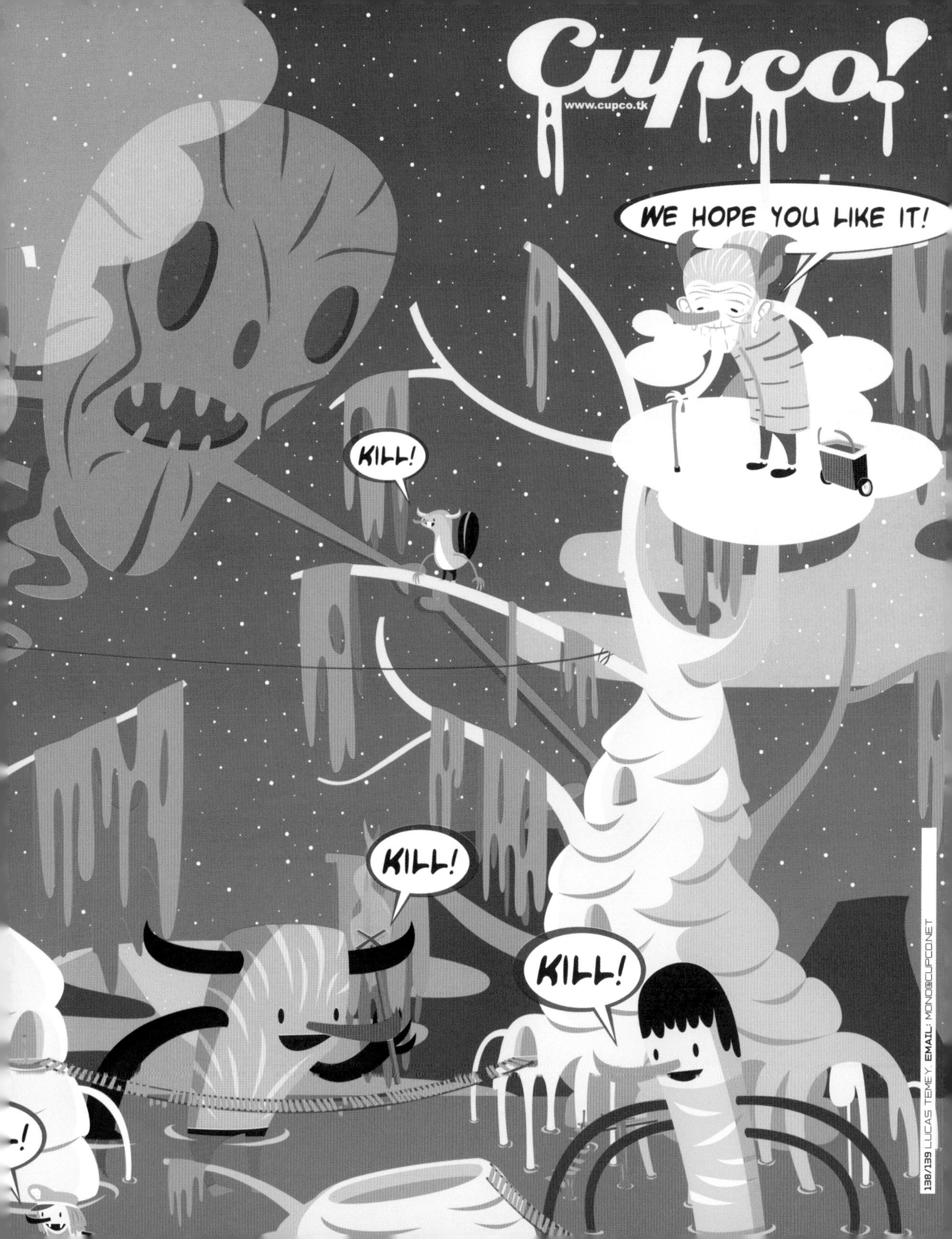

138/139 LUCAS TEMEY. EMAIL: MONO@CUPCO.NET

 VICKI WONG (MEOMI DESIGN). EMAIL: INFO@MEOMI.COM

gris

Art exhibit, web related work & personal playground
Depthflow.net™

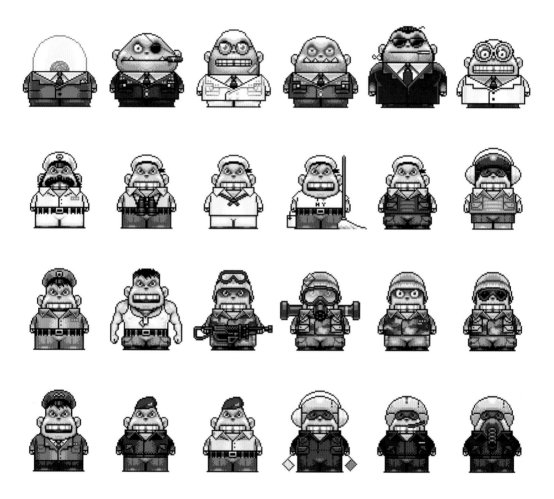

George

Frank

Bruce

William

File not found!

John

Michael

Harry

Peter

Bob

Arthur

Joseph

John John

Bill

Ron

Elliot

Fernando

Ronald

Clark

Gennaro

Paul

Sammy Jr.

Mohammed

Alfred

 TOTTO RENNA. EMAIL: INFO@SUPERTOTTO.COM

te voy a pinchar,

trinchar

y zampar

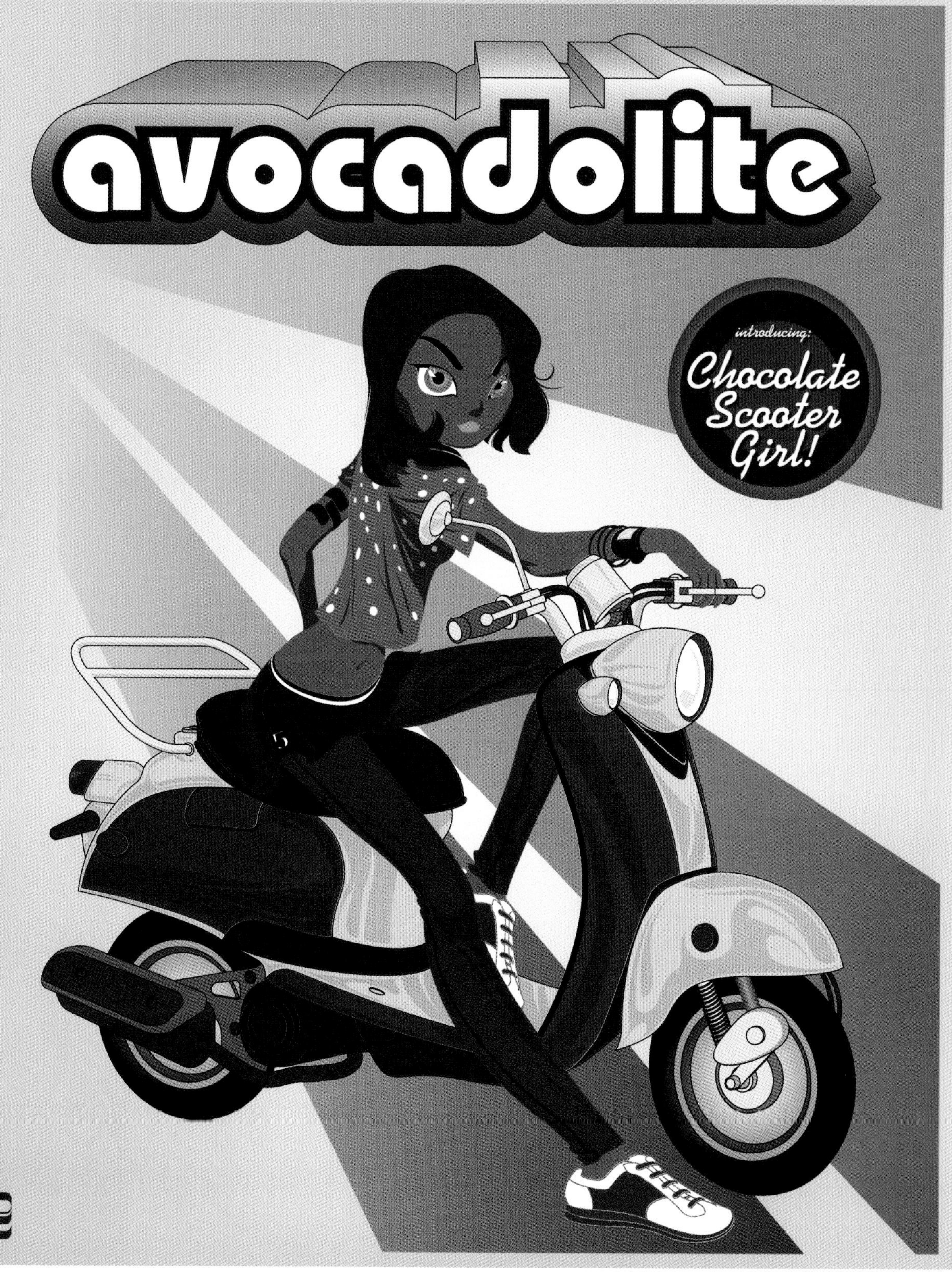

avocadolite

introducing:
Chocolate
Scooter
Girl!

Illustration by
Russell Tate

bomb

B O M B

Triple J

The
9th
PLANET

SOFTWARE

m BOMB

Illogical Solutions

HERA:V2.1-PAUL.YOUNG

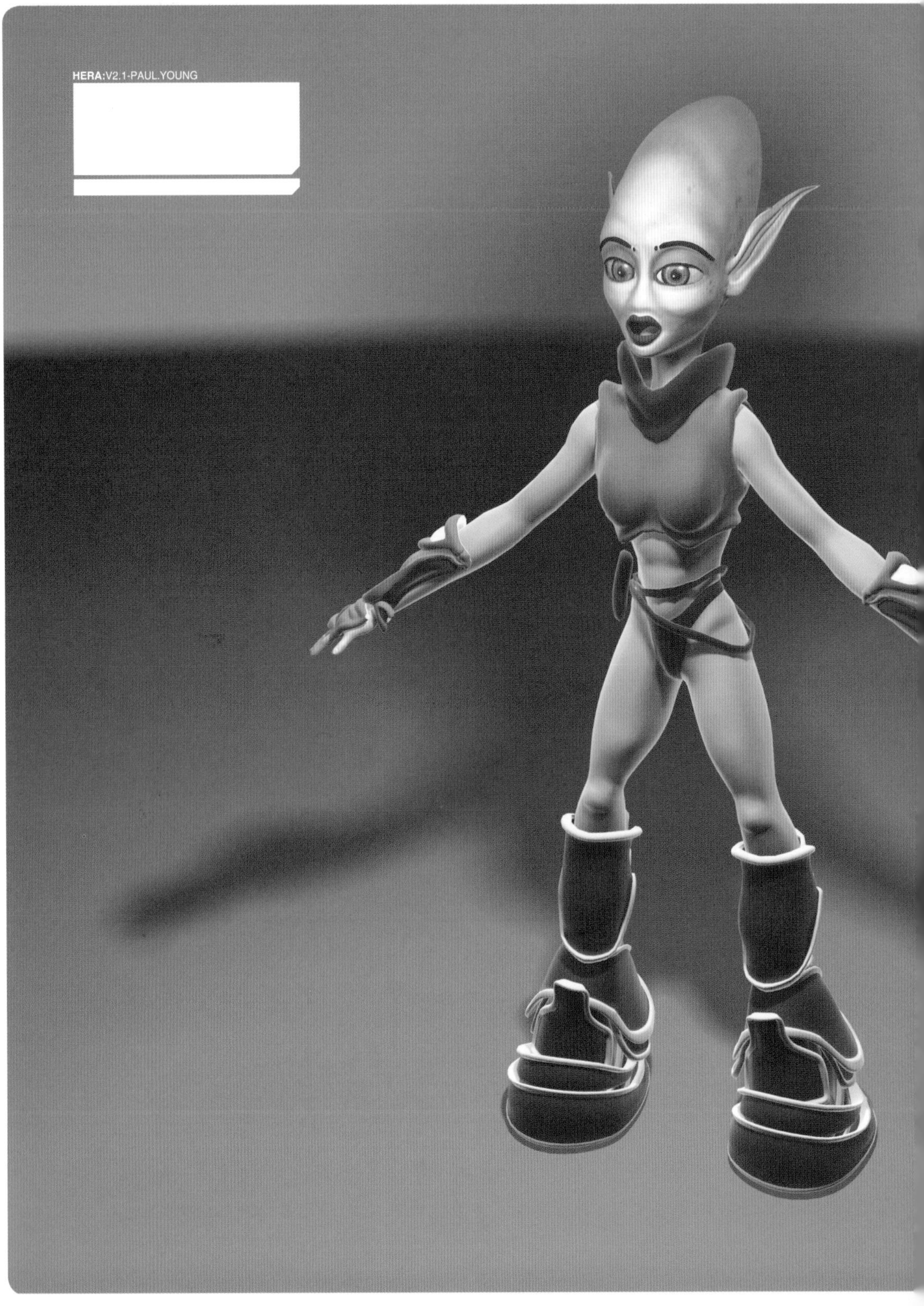

ENPH:V3.4-PAUL_YOUNG

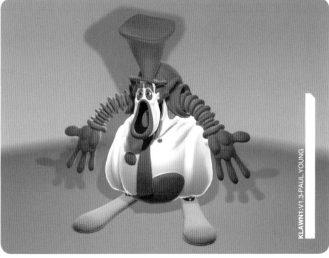
KLAWN1:V1.3-PAUL_YOUNG

KLAWN2:V4.1-PAUL_YOUNG

PUSHBAK
REF#003.PSD/DIAGNOSTIC
FREEWARE/OPN SRC

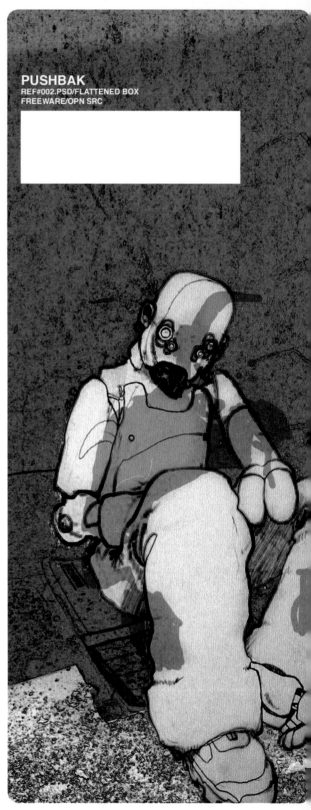

PUSHBAK
REF#002.PSD/FLATTENED BOX
FREEWARE/OPN SRC

PUSHBAK
REF#004.PSD/LOOKING UP
FREEWARE/OPN SRC

I WISH I HAD A BABY
ELEPHANT

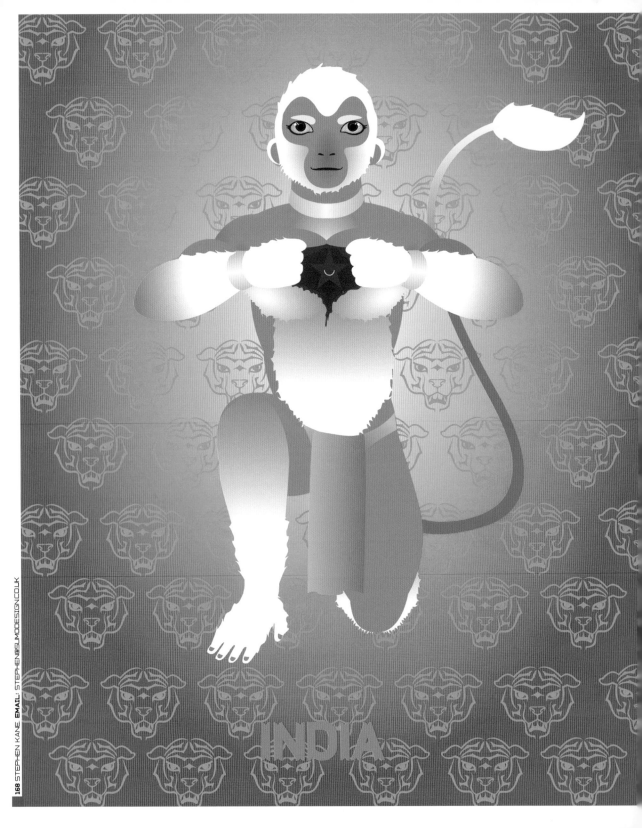

india

 STEFANIE KOERNER **EMAIL**: MONOCHROMB@GMX.DE

TAKE YOUR PICTURE HERE

Junichi.Kato.CMD9-2.

Junichi.Kato.CMD9-3.

Junichi.Kato.CMD9-1.

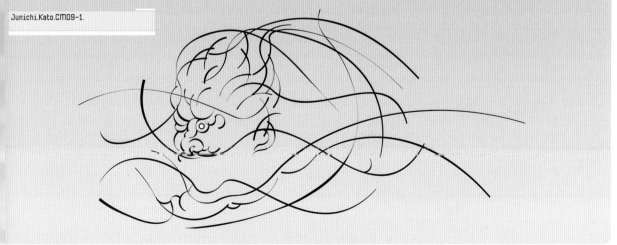

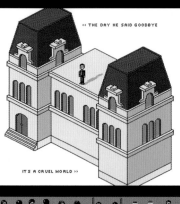

‹‹ THE DAY HE SAID GOODBYE

IT'S A CRUEL WORLD ››

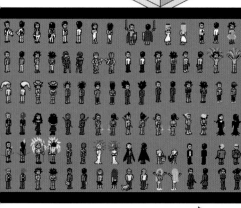

SEWING MACHINE

STEREO SYSTEM

WASHING MACHINE

NEOPOD HOME APPLIANCE RANGE

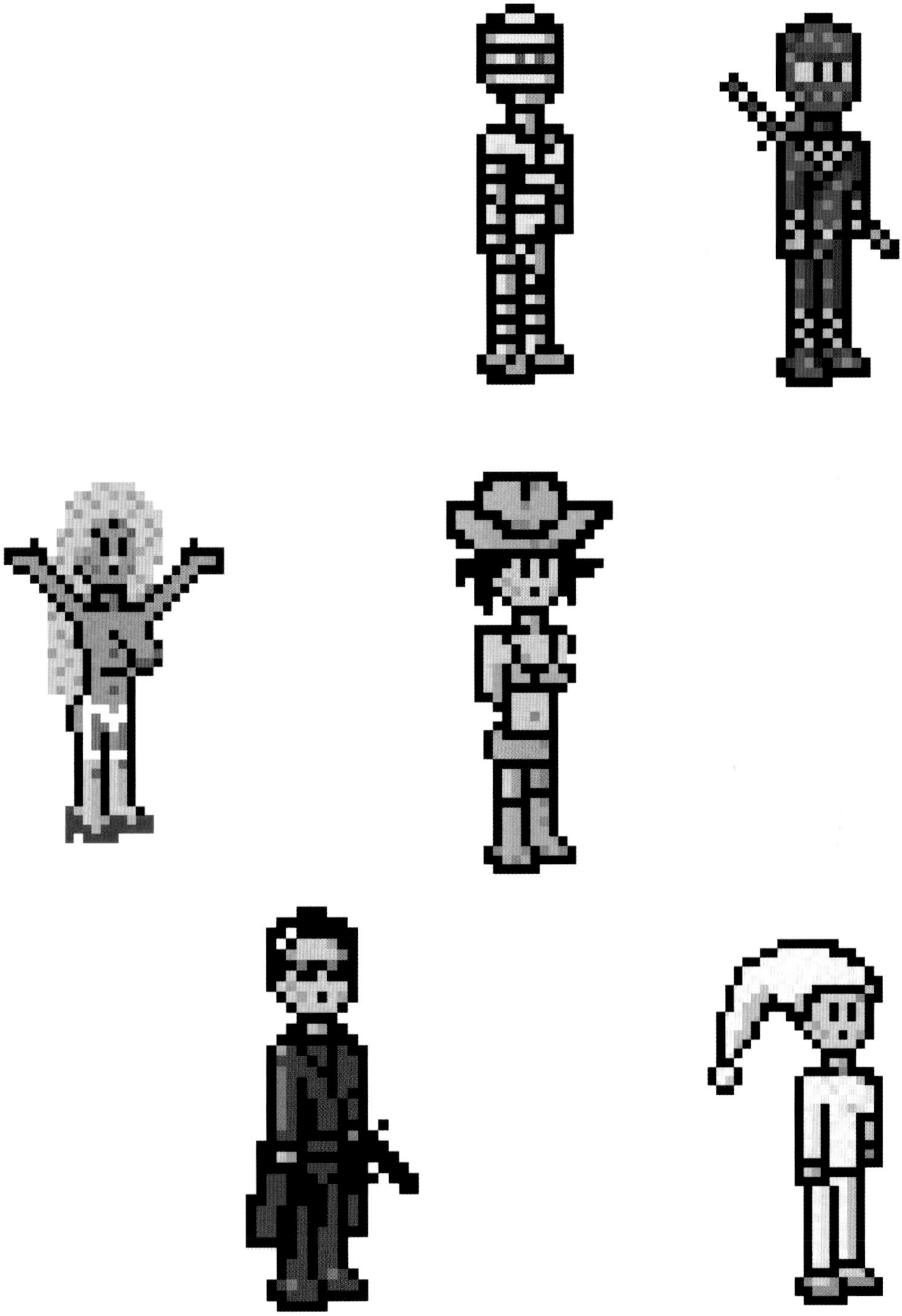

 EMAIL: MAIL@PEJOT.COM

NON-HUMANWARE

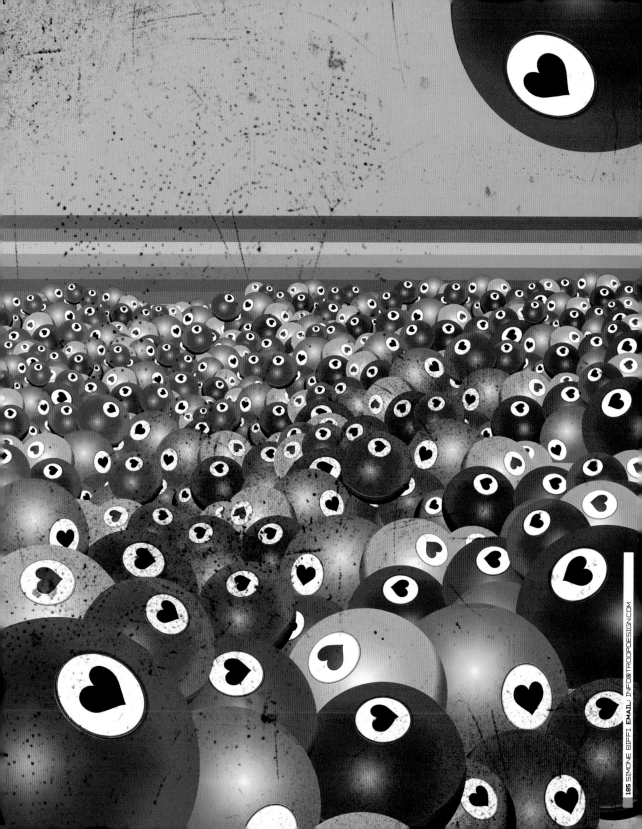

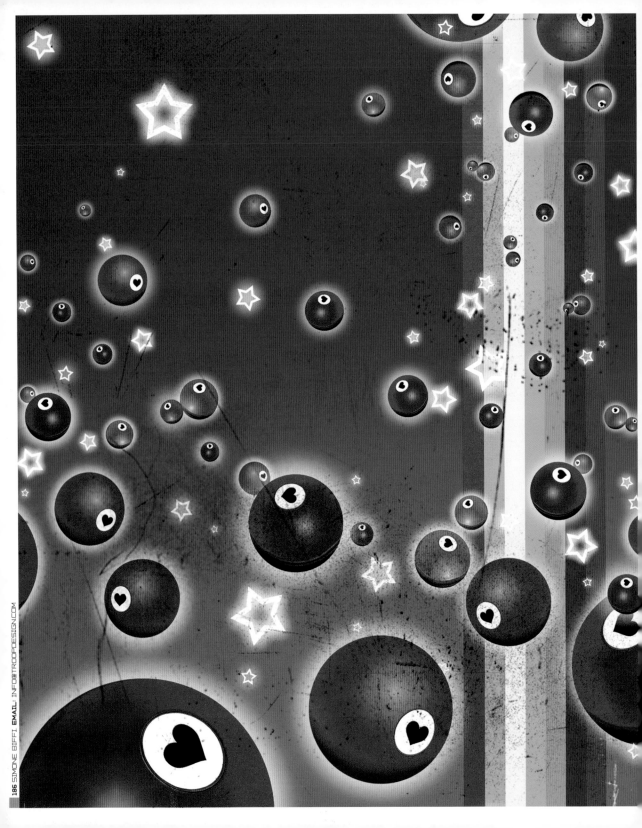

MISUNDERSTOOD

187 | SIMONE BIFFI EMAIL: INFO@TROOPDESIGN.COM

SN
N
NT
RC_ia

I'm looking for it, and I can't find it, nor can I remember the name of it.
it was made with seaweed.

I used a facial cleanser that I'd bought from a vegetarian heath food store a while ago,
and when I went back to the store to buy another bottle they said they didn't have it in stock any more.
it's the best thing I've ever used because it doesn't dry my face out,
but it cleans it gently.

Plnts in the nvrnmnt

As a critical part of the ecosystem, plants provide oxygen for organisms to survive. They are able to reduce the
problem of pollution, by using carbon dioxide. Plants are also the basis of most food webs as producers of food for
herbivores and ultimately carnivores. Plants also provide shelter for animals, clean and filter water and help

see WD

prevent soil erosion.

007 .spnsh G

Its composition is a meta concept which can be
applied to any medium or any experience.

Momentum: And
quality is a well-balanced
combination of ingredients,
mixtures and scents.
Complexity does not
necessarily create completeness.
If merely distracts from the essence,
covering up the truth. If there is any. Simplicity is clean
and direct. The right amount of salt makes an egg taste
perfect, considering the conditions. All depends on when and where.
Timing is crucial and simplicity is excellence. Quality. The quality of talent lies
within its limitations, not within its possibilities. Dealing with physical limitations and
reality, the professional designer often has to be inventive and
improvise to solve a problem within a limited timeframe. He needs to be practical and efficient.
He needs to know what to look for, but more importantly, when to stop.

Revolution: A definition of typography is obsolete. The institution of type is abolished. Its power is
defeated. Since its digital manifestation, type has been outlawed. Type is nothing more than
a tone, a sound, a noise. Parts and details are ticks, squeaks and vibrations. Letters,
glyphs or characters have lost their intentional meaning and become transparent
notations. New forms will be defined by The Remix.

Articulate: Visual articulation is a downright representation of meaning. Depending on the
time, place and tools, any idea will find a specific form. An image can only look the
way it is at the moment of its appearance. Expression of language depends on
the need to use it. There is always a particular and suitable way for individual
expression to communicate. It is the precipitation of a process on a specific
moment, an enumeration of vision and opinion, relevance of purpose,
cultural reference, experience and insights, and the exploration of freedom,
within limitations of time, production and techniques.

Limitation: Errors break down the predictable, the expected and obvious.
An error is not necessarily a failure. With errors the unforeseen results
will be surprising and might have an even stranger impact. Errors will
confront us with the physical and mental limitations of possibilities. There
is a beauty in errors, as they shift reality from its predefined conditions
and conventions. Errors are the beauty of imperfectness.

Log Out:
I see you behind the glass
of the digital transporter. You not
here you here. I touch you
on the screen in between
where we meet.
Your lips are moving, but your
voice fades away. Saying
that you want me. I still
can't read your lips.
You there. My eyes are
closed. I feel you all
over. Your absence
doesn't need
a picture.

TIMID St

Once down there, all sounds
are cut off. Overhead travel paths
vanish in the thin air. Motorized
river noises crumble away.
Moving at a steady pace.
The silence overwhelms. Only
the sound of breathing
and the scraping steps
on the trail. Everything
is gone. No birds, no
humans, no cars,
no cities. A breeze
causes a
shiver.

Orch d

Composure:
Looking for the form.
Composure. Like a mould
to pour into. An exact
image of the shape is
generated in the mind. From
an internal viewpoint observing
its motion. It all starts with the initial position. Its initial
balance. Placing the point of gravity right there, where its
power stretches in an upward rush as flattening out, with a circular
scaler. For a millisecond the eye meets the contact point of energise and
de-energise. The diagonal shift will securely strike the press, radiant target.
Execution: When the space is empty, the mind is blank.

Response: Once down there, all sounds are cut off. Overhead travel paths vanish in the thin air.
Motorized river noises crumble away r. Moving at a steady pace, the silence overwhelms. Only
the sound of breathing and the scraping steps on the trail. Everything is gone. No birds, no humans.

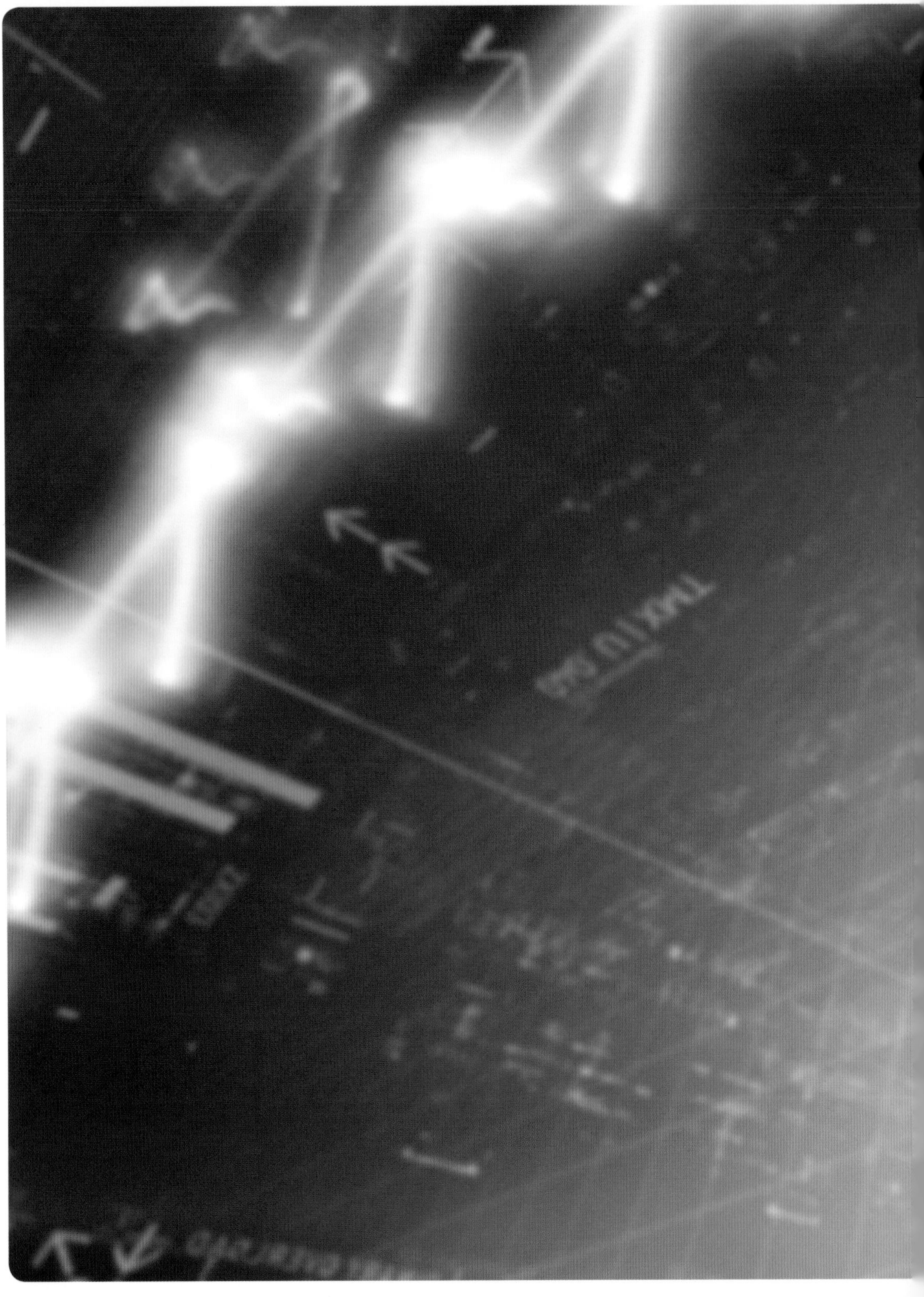

MAYUMI TAKAMI **EMAIL**: TAKAMIX@POP16.ODN.NE.JP

FICTITIOUS SCULPTURE
IT HAS GENTLE CURVES AND COLORS. I WANNA LET EVERYONE FEEL GENTLE BY SEEING IT.

CREATED BY MAYUMI TAKAMI "NONAME DESIGN" http://takamix0925.cool.ne.jp/

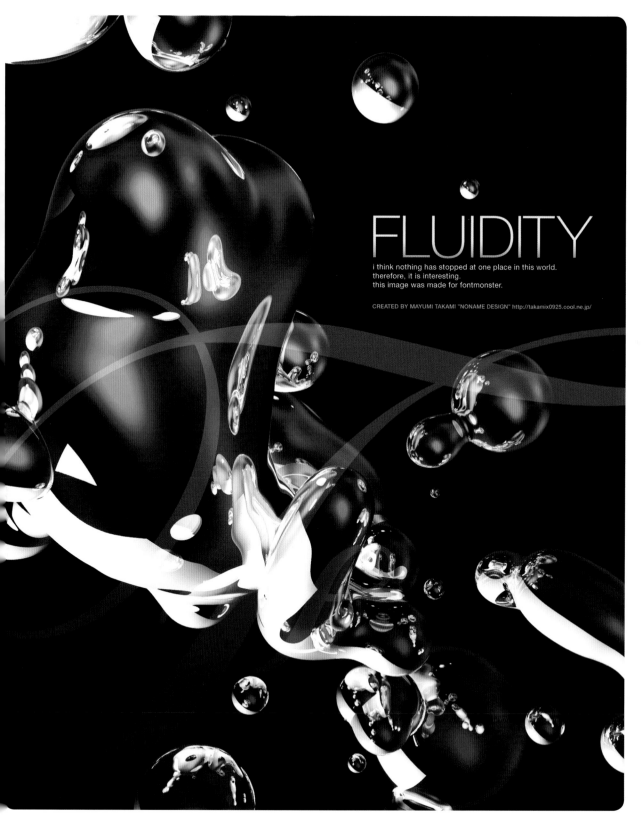

FLUIDITY

i think nothing has stopped at one place in this world.
therefore, it is interesting.
this image was made for fontmonster.

CREATED BY MAYUMI TAKAMI "NONAME DESIGN" http://takamix0925.cool.ne.jp/

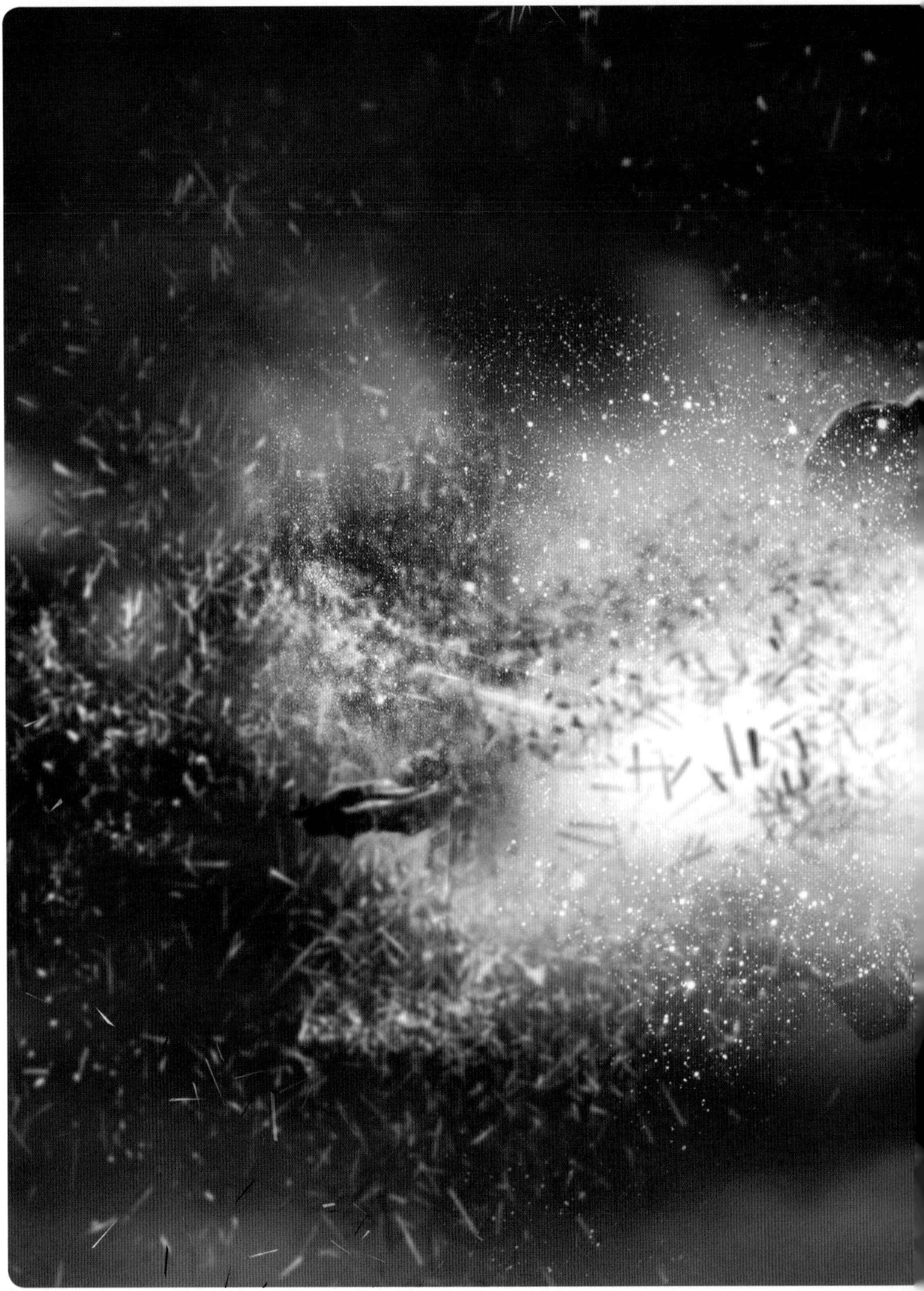

mess

 JOEL EVEY: **EMAIL**: JOEL@MIKRONIZED.COM

blight

622
Prototype XG-621

602
Cybernetics CY-5505

Connector

ATROPINE
374

Prototype XG-621

BIOSTIMULE XW02

Architectural Detail N°01

01 Backside View

ExtremeHabitat

Other Names QB IMPF, isopropoxymethylphosphoryl fluoride methylphosphonofluoridic acid isopropyl ester MF1 phosphine oxide, fluoroisopropoxymethyl Sarin II T-144 T-2106 TL 1618 Trilone 46

02 Top View

03 Left View

04 Custom View

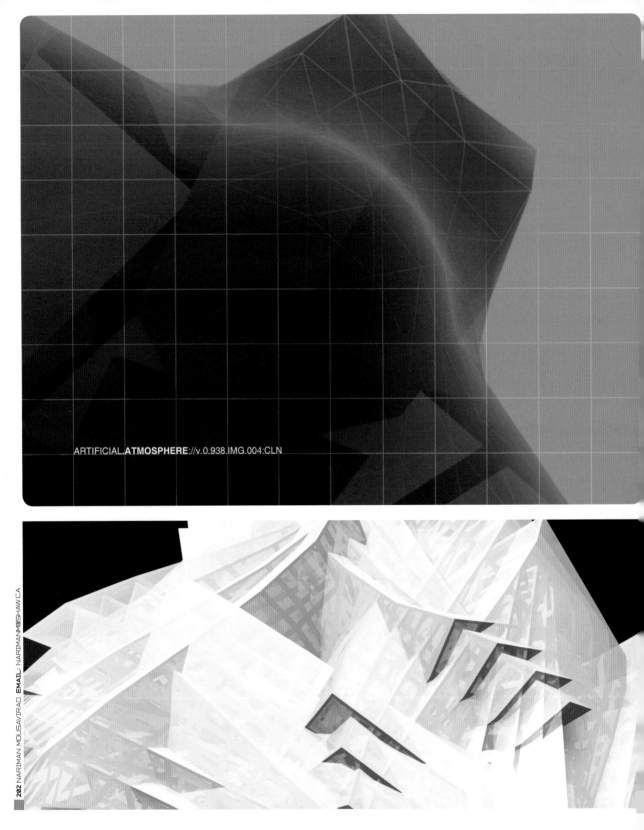

ARTIFICIAL.**ATMOSPHERE**://v.0.938.IMG.004:CLN

LUST.COLOUR
ARTIFICIALATMOSPHERE

203 NARIMAN MOUSAVIRAD EMAIL: NARIMAN@SHAW.CA

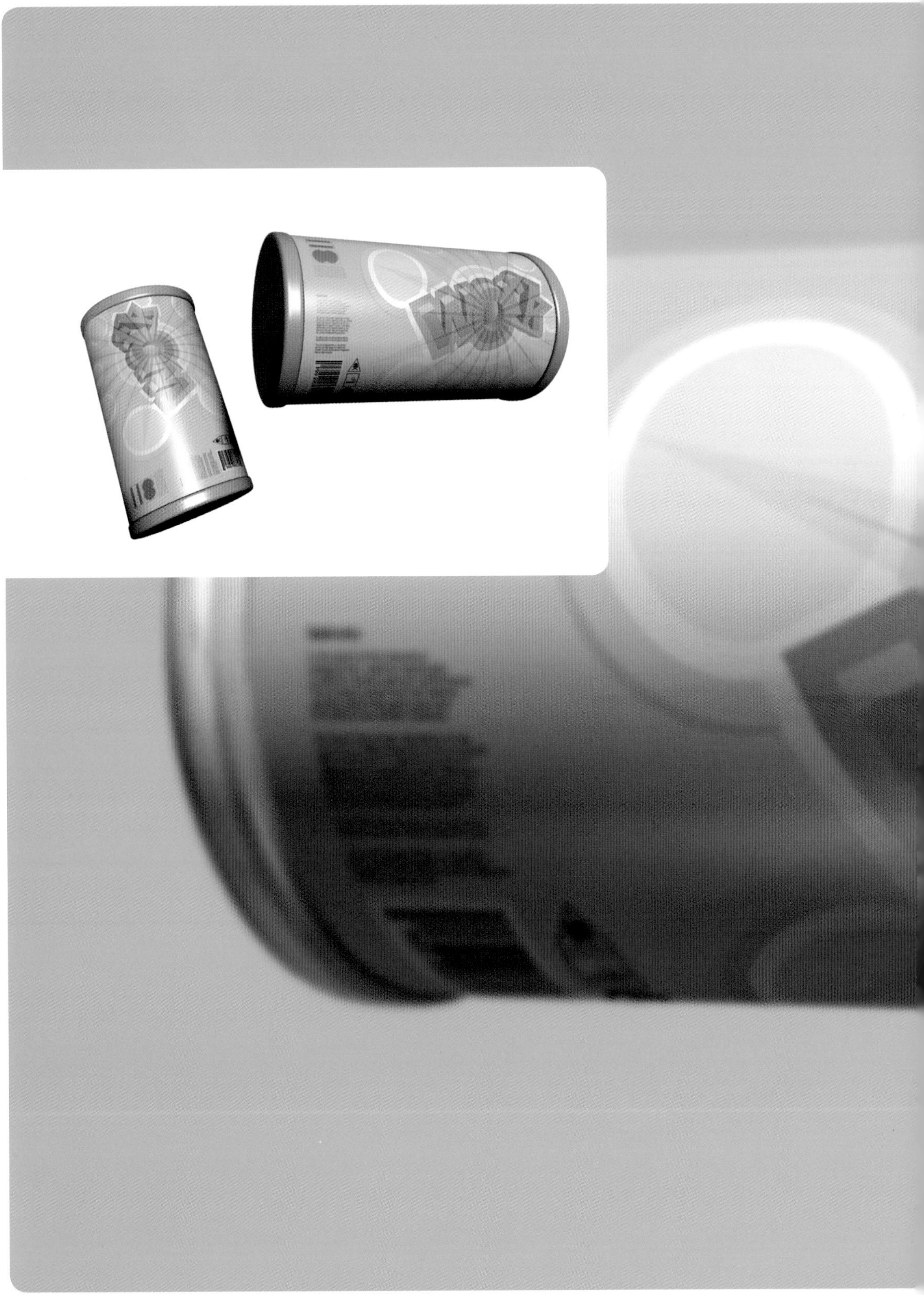

scratchware

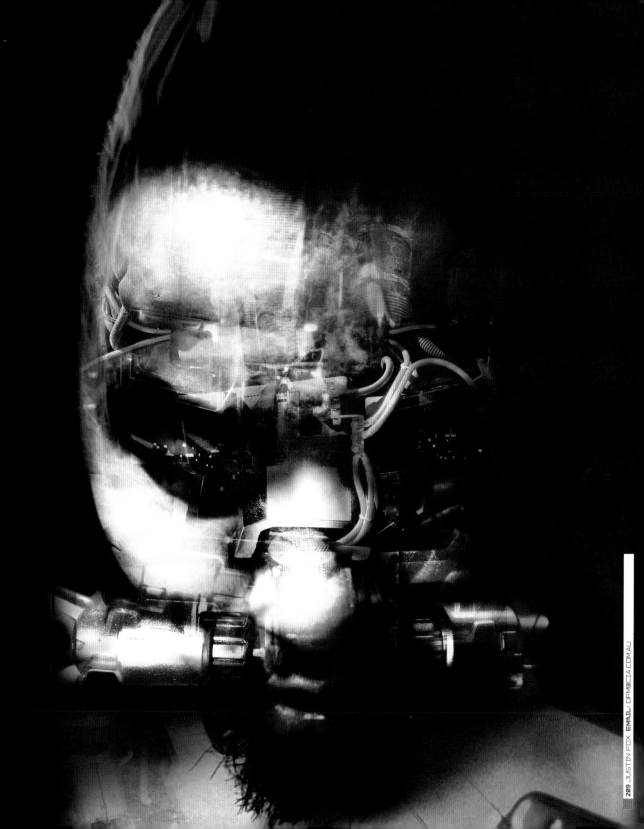

BACKGROUND OBJECTS: MASA DINGBATS: DAVID LUSCOMBE

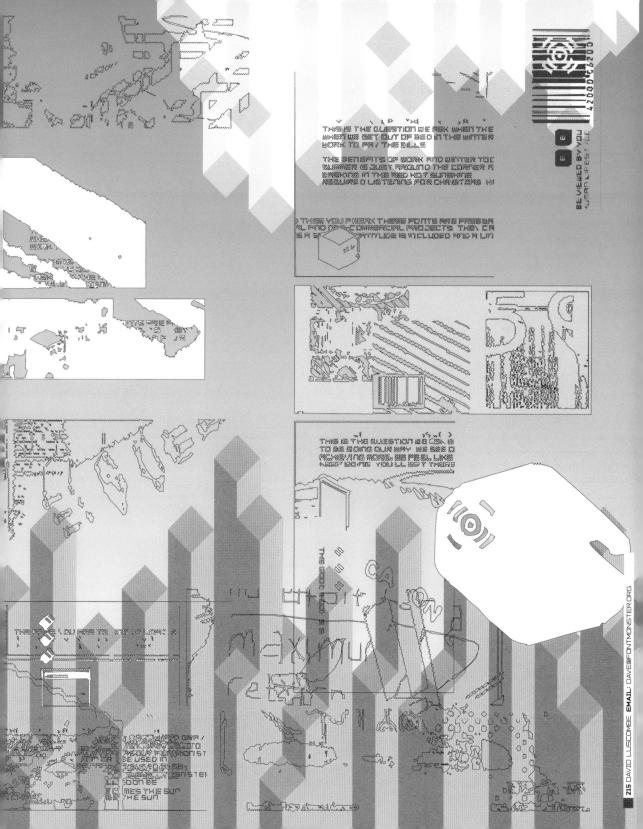

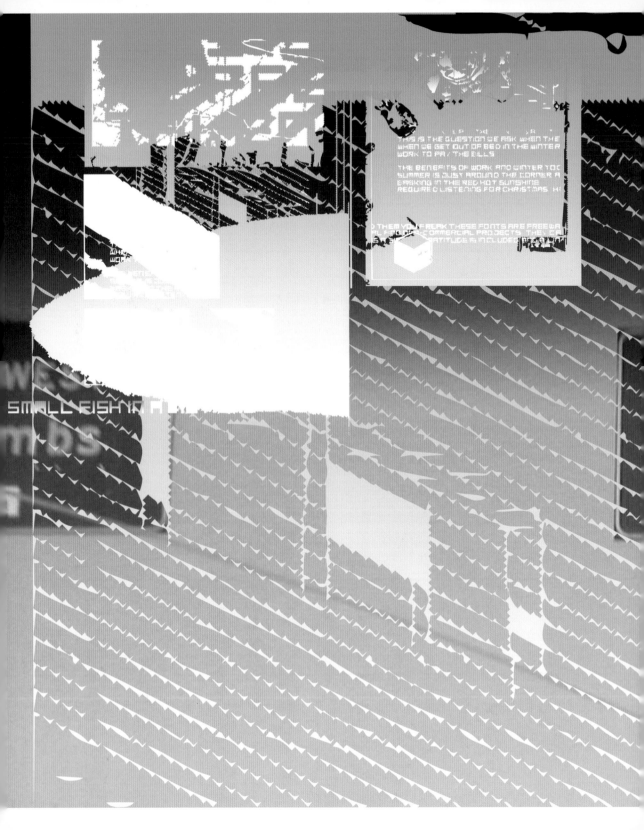

EAST
Parksville

 EMAIL: JMR@ROCCUZZO.COM

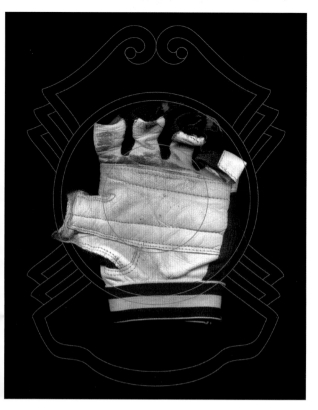

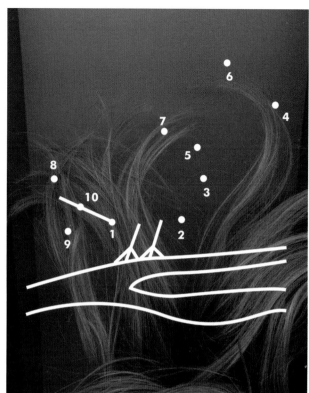

Schwester mir eine angenehme Unterhaltung verschaffen, die eine ... indem ... und doch so ganz unschuldig?

... ene Empfindu... ... etwas ist de... ... ... so wenig lächerlich... ... ... nicht mehr ein bißchen klug, wie gibt das ... so gar nicht mehr ... ... so genießt, die Gegenwärtige genießen, und das Vergangene soll mir vergangen sein. Gewiß, du hast recht, Bester, der Schmerzen wären minder unter den Menschen, wenn sie nicht ... ... um sich so geschäftig mit der Einbildungskraft sich beschäftigten, die Erinnerungen des vergangenen Übels zurückzurufen, eher als eine gleichgültige Gegenwart zu ertragen.

Goethe - Die Leiden des jungen Werther - 1774

... je me suis couché de bonne heure. Parfois, à peine ma bougie éteinte, mes yeux se fermaient si vite que je n'avais pas le temps de me dire : « Je m'endors. » Et, une demi-heure après, la pensée qu'il était temps de chercher le sommeil m'éveillait ; ... ... je n'avais pas cessé en dormant de faire des réflexions sur ce que je venais de lire, mais ces réflexions avaient pris un tour un peu particulier ; ... ... semblait que j'étais moi-même ce dont parlait l'ouvrage : une église, un quatuor, la rivalité de François Ier et de Charles-Quint. Cette croyance survivait pendant quelques ... ... des à mon réveil ;

... commen... lait à me ... vei... l'intelli... ... comme apr... la métempsycose les pensées d'une existence antérieure ; le sujet du livre se détachait de moi, ... de m'y appliquer ou non ; ... ... je recourais la vue et j'étais bien étonné de trouver autour de moi une obscurité, douce et reposante pour mes yeux, mais peut-être plus encore pour mon esprit, à qui elle apparaissait comme une chose sans cause, ...

... ... vraiment obscure." (M. Proust - Du côté de chez Swann - 1913

A z

Hbit

(0_0)
for monitor only

9pixel

```
 !"#$%&'()*+,-./0123456789:;
<=>?@ABCDEFGHIJKLMNOPQRSTUVW
XYZ[\]^_`abcdefghijklmnopqrs
tuvwxyz{|}~ ÄÅÇÉÑÖÜáàâääåçéè
êëíììîñóòôöõúùûü †°¢£§•¶ß®©™´¨
≠ÆØœ±≤≥¥µ∂Σ∏π∫ªºΩæø¿¡¬√ƒ≈∆«»
»… ÀÃÕŒœ––""''÷◊ÿŸ⁄¤‹›ﬁﬂ‡·‚
‰ÂÊÁËÈÍÎÏÌÓÔ×ÒÚÛÙ¹˜¯˘˙˚¸˝˛ˇ
```

10pixel

```
 !"#$%&'()*+,-./0123456789
:;<=>?@ABCDEFGHIJKLMNOPQRS
TUVWXYZ[\]^_`abcdefghijklm
nopqrstuvwxyz{|}~ ÄÅÇÉÑÖÜá
àâääåçéèêëíììîñóòôöõúùûü †°
¢£§•¶ß®©™´¨≠ÆØœ±≤≥¥µ∂Σ∏π∫ª
ºΩæø¿¡¬√ƒ≈∆«»… ÀÃÕŒœ––""''
÷◊ÿŸ⁄¤‹›ﬁﬂ‡·‚‰ÂÊÁËÈÍÎÏÌÓÔ
×ÒÚÛÙ¹˜¯˘˙˚¸˝˛ˇ
```

12pixel

```
 !"#$%&'()*+,-./01234
56789:;<=>?@ABCDEFGHI
JKLMNOPQRSTUVWXYZ[\]^
_`abcdefghijklmnopqrs
tuvwxyz{|}~ ÄÅÇÉÑÖÜáà
âääåçéèêëíììîñóòôöõúù
ûü †°¢£§•¶ß®©™´¨≠ÆØœ±≤
≥¥µ∂Σ∏π∫ªºΩæø¿¡¬√ƒ≈∆
«»… ÀÃÕŒœ––""''÷◊ÿŸ⁄¤‹
›ﬁﬂ‡·‚‰ÂÊÁËÈÍÎÏÌÓÔ×Ò
ÚÛÙ¹˜¯˘˙˚¸˝˛ˇ
```

NONE IS

I AM NOT AN ENEMY

أنا ...

أنا لست

أنا عدوًا لست [I AM NOT AN ENEMY]

Born in BEYROUTH

Tomorrow, we won't be judged based on where we come from,
we won't be stereotyped, we won't be treated based on our nationalities...
We won't need visas to go from a place to another.
We won't need passports, or other meaningless booklets and papers.
We will all be able to go around freely in our world.
We will accept and coexist with other communities,
and will all be treated as equal and similar human beings.

I am born in Beirut. I am proudly an Arab. I am not an enemy.
And I am waiting for a better tomorrow...

TAREK ATRISSI

toydrum
; wild phonotronics!

feel...

clients

orm follows

madison NY

till do. Not in this case

these are my thoughts, fragmented on this air

Dedicated to my mother, who

passed away

Untill I heard the news my mom died. All that seemed beautifull was now irrelevant. NY was turned upsidedown from one moment to the other

It is a difficult decision to make layouts about yourself. Can you reward? I still do. Not in this case though. Form follow function and to some clients? I will talk perhaps.

Or something light, designs, trends. Another, perhaps. But this time I could wait. I then really stick to just doing something safe, all of the paper. If you've got nothing to say. Expensive? Very superficial. But its disturbing.

When walking somewhere
with my camera and notebook
I ~~follow~~ rest occasionally to
sketch or take pictures.

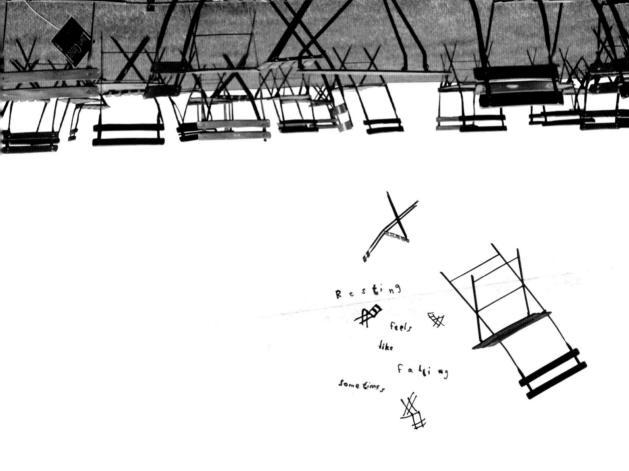

Resting feels like falling sometimes

titulo: Mandala

descripcion:

↓ENTRAR

09

ABRUMADO

ENTRAR

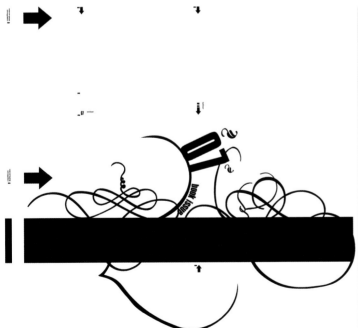

231 IVAN IVANOFF EMAIL: AVATAR@I2OFF.ORG

MAURICIO SANCHEZ. **EMAIL:** M@TELETYPO.COM

J. HURTIG. **EMAIL:** JUHANA.HURTIG@LUUKKU.COM

FONS SCHIEDON. **EMAIL:** OFFICE@FONSTV.NL

WE DANSDEN
ALSOF ER
GEEN
MORGEN
WAS

BACKGROUND PHOTO: ROBERT POWER. **EMAIL:** ROBERT@BALANCEIMAGES.ORG

SAMBA

NoT DEAD

NOEL ROSA, NELSON CAVAQUINHO, PAULINHO DA VI
ZECA PAGODINHO,
BEZERRA DA SILVA, CLARA NUNES,
CARTOLA, JOAO NOGUEIRA, CANDEIA,
VEL
GUARDA DA PORTELA
NELSON SARGENTO, etc

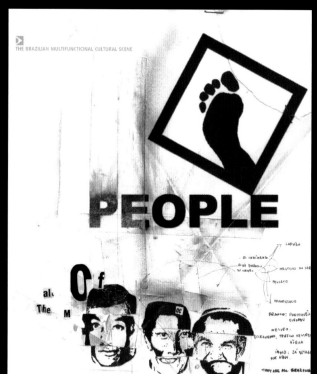

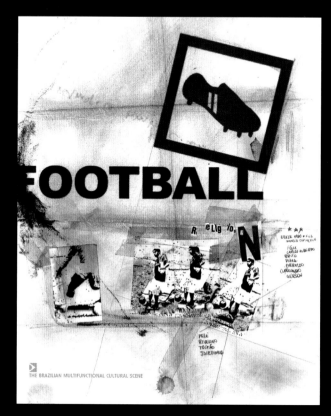

ARTIFICIALATMOSPHERE

index

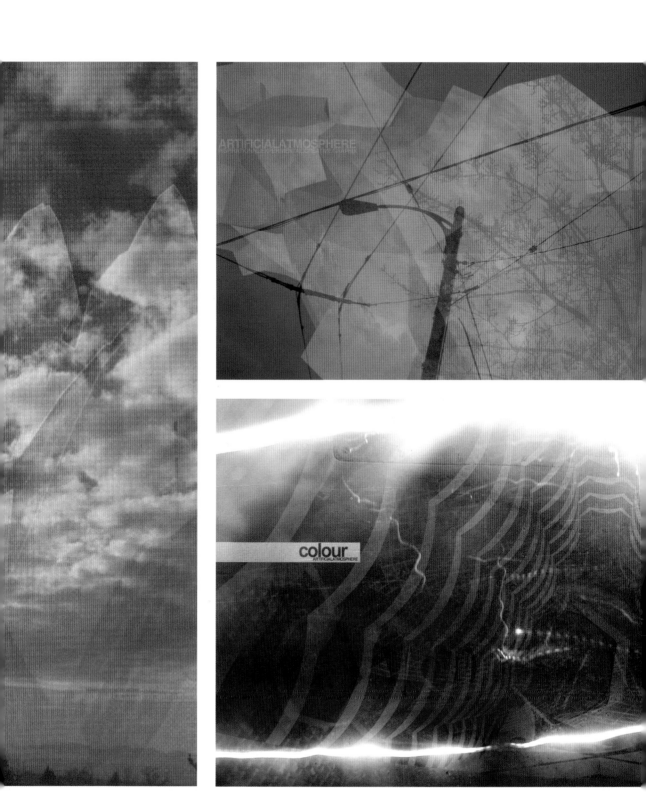

ARTIFICIALATMOSPHERE

colour
ARTIFICIALATMOSPHERE

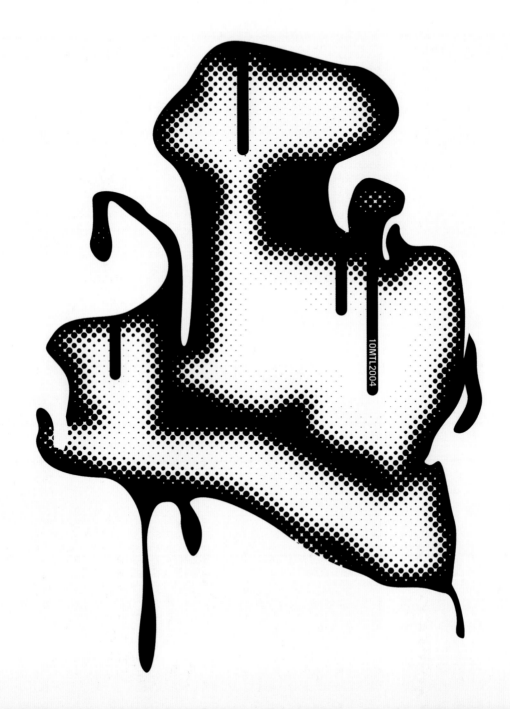

10MTL2004

CRIME

tenmetal

wow!

insect

piscina
chlorine: 1 ppm / ph: 7.2 / humidity: 98% / temperature: 28C°

249 OL3 EMAIL: OL3@OL3.IT

HERE IN NEW YORK CITY SUMMER I
EVEN INSIDE THE SUBWAY. CARS WI
FATAL, SPECIALLY WHEN HALF OF T
VERY LITTLE ABOUT DEODORANT. JU

A KILLER. THE HEAT WILL FRY YOU

H NO AIR CONDITIONING CAN BE

E POPULATION KNOWS NOTHING OR

ST ANOTHER DAY IN PARADISE....

DECONSTRUCTED
WORLD

(where were you?)

DIGITAL FRAME - XPAN 24

DIGITAL FRAME - XPAN 23

238

237

236

ELEMENTS 01
THE FIRE

0250°K

0500°K

1000°K

1500°K

LINK5 DOT COM DESIGN

EST. 2001

...ones A... ...res, S... ...34
Colección ...). Printed in Spain

España 0,25c

DMSTK

Pr...da... ...tos los d... reser...

index / contacts

■ FONTWARE

▓ VECTORWARE

▓ HUMANWARE

▓ SUB-HUMANWARE

▓ NON-HUMANWARE

■ SCRATCHWARE

■ DATA DVD

Adam Hayes
Place: England
Web: www.identikal.com
E-mail: adam@identikal.com
Section medals: ▓ ■ **Page No:** 132

Alex Dukal
Place: Argentina
Web: www.adukal.com
E-mail: adukal@adukal.com
Section medals: ▓ ■ **Page No:** 157, 158

Andrea Volpicelli
Place: Italy
Phone: +39 (0)335 349 505
Web: www.andreavolpicelli.com
E-mail: andrea@andreavolpicelli.com
Section medals: ▓ ▓ ■ **Page No:** 93, 246, 247

Andrew Wilson
Place: USA
Web: www.filter9.com
www.andrewwilsondesign.com
E-mail: f9@filter9.com
Section medals: ■ ■ **Page No:** 45

Anna Augul
Place: USA
E-mail: aaugul@monashdigital.com
Section medals: ▓ ■ **Page No:** 130, 131

Ari Widjanarko
Place: Singapore
Web: www.pericraft.com
www.avocadolite.com
www.yobotica.com
E-mail: info@pericraft.com
Section medals: ▓ ■ **Page No:** 159

Arjen Noordeman
Place: The Netherlands
Web: www.noordeman.com
E-mail: arjen@noordeman.com
Section medals: ■ ■ **Page No:** 16, 17

BaseV
Place: Brazil
Web: http://basev.has.it
E-mail: basev@email.com
Section medals: ■ ■ **Page No:** 29, 30, 31

Ben Morris
Place: Scotland
Phone: +44 (0)7880 574 658
Web: www.ben.morris.btinternet.co.uk
E-mail: ben.morris@btinternet.com
Section medals: ■

Bernd Sperber
Place: Germany
Web: www.footo.de
E-mail: sperber@footo.de
Section medals: ■

Kjetil Vatne
Place: Norway
Phone: +47 975 02 599
Web: www.kvad.com
E-mail: vatne@kvad.com
Section medals: ■ ■ ■ **Page No:** 30, 31, 174

Kwan Li
Place: England
E-mail: kwan@fontmonster.org
Section medals: ■

Leri Greer
Place: USA
E-mail: leri@pushback.com
Section medals: ■ ■ **Page No:** 166, 167

Liam Wolf
Place: Australia
Web: www.neopod.net
E-mail: mail@neopod.net
Section medals: ■ ■ ■ **Page No:** 133, 180, 181

Luca Marchettoni
Place: Italy
Web: www.w3d.it
E-mail: luca@w3d.it
Section medals: ■

Lucas Temby
Place: Japan
Web: www.cupco.net
E-mail: momo@cupco.net
Section medals: ■ ■ **Page No:** 137, 138, 139

Luiggi Tapuch / Red X Design
Place: USA
Phone: +1 917 696 7222
Web: www.redxdesign.com
E-mail: info@redxdesign.com
Section medals: ■ ■ **Page No:** 244, 245

Luke Prowse
Place: England
Web: www.stereotypography.com
E-mail: luke@stereotypography.com
Section medals: ■ ■ **Page No:** 232, 233

Marcel Eichner
Place: Germany
Web: www.ephigenia.de
E-mail: love@ephigenia.de
Section medals: ■ ■
Page No: 118, 119, 120, 121, 122, 123

Marcelo Baldin
Place: Brazil
Phone: +55 11 8121 5445
Web: www.combustion.ws
E-mail: combustion@combustion.ws
Section medals: ■ ■ **Page No:** 91

Marco Alessi / Floorless
Place: Studio 202 The Saga Centre 326 Kesnal Road
London W10 5BZ England
Web: www.floorless.com
E-mail: info@floorless.com
Section medals: ■ ■ **Page No:** 96, 97

Marco Antonio Morales
Place: Barcelona Spain
Phone: +34 647 217 667
Web: www.antidisseny.com
www.marcoantonio.org
E-mail: marco@antidisseny.com
Section medals: ■ ■ **Page No:** 44, 45

Martin Woodtli
Place: Switzerland
Web: www.woodt.li
E-mail: martin@woodt.li
Section medals: ■

MASA
Place: Av. Araure Qta. Marel
Chuao El Cafetal Caracas 1061 Venezuela
Phone: +58 212 991 25 85
+58 212 991 51 91
Web: www.masa.com.ve
E-mail: info@masa.com.ve
Section medals: ■ ■ ■
Page No: 78, 79, 80, 81, 82, 83, 84, 85, 210, 211

Mauricio Sanchez
Place: USA
Phone: +1 703 869 9273
Web: www.teletypo.com
E-mail: m@teletypo.com
Section medals: ■ ■ **Page No:** 235

Max Kisman
Place: USA
Web: www.maxkisman.com
E-mail: maxk@maxkisman.com
Section medals: ■ ■ **Page No:** 22, 24, 25, 26, 27

Mayumi Takami
Place: Japan
Web: http://takamix0925.cool.ne.jp
E-mail: takamix@pop16.odn.ne.jp
Section medals: ■ ■ **Page No:** 192, 193

Melissa Crowley
Place: USA
Web: www.redbean.com
E-mail: melissa@redbean.com
Section medals: ■

Milan Zrnic
Place: USA
E-mail: mil@fontlover.com
Section medals: ■ ■ **Page No:** 90